On
Manners

Many otherwise enlightened people often dismiss etiquette as a trivial subject or—worse yet—as nothing but a disguise for moral hypocrisy or unjust social hierarchies. Such sentiments either mistakenly assume that most manners merely frame the "real issues" of any interpersonal exchange or are the ugly vestiges of outdated, unfair social arrangements. But in On Manners, Karen Stohr turns the tables on these easy prejudices, demonstrating that the scope of manners is much broader than most people realize and that manners lead directly to the roots of enduring ethical questions. Stohr suggests that though manners are mostly conventional, they are nevertheless authoritative insofar as they are a primary means by which we express moral attitudes and commitments and carry out important moral goals.

Drawing primarily on Aristotle and Kant and with references to a wide range of cultural examples—from Jane Austen's Pride and Prejudice to Larry David's Curb Your Enthusiasm—the author ultimately concludes that good manners are essential to moral character.

Karen Stohr is Associate Professor of Philosophy at Georgetown University in Washington D.C., where she is also a Senior Research Scholar in the Kennedy Institute of Ethics.

Praise for the series

'. . . allows a space for distinguished thinkers to write about their passions.'

The Philosophers' Magazine

'. . . deserve high praise.'

Boyd Tonkin, The Independent (UK)

'This is clearly an important series. I look forward to receiving future volumes.'

Frank Kermode, author of Shakespeare's Language

'both rigorous and accessible'

Humanist News

'the series looks superb'

Quentin Skinner

'. . . an excellent and beautiful series.'

Ben Rogers, author of A.J. Ayer: A Life

'Routledge's *Thinking in Action* series is the theory junkie's answer to the eminently pocketable Penguin 60s series.'

Mute Magazine (UK)

'Routledge's new series, *Thinking in Action*, brings philosophers to our aid . . .'

The Evening Standard (UK)

'. . . a welcome series by Routledge'

Bulletin of Science, Technology and Society (Can)

'Routledge's innovative new *Thinking in Action* series takes the concept of philosophy a step further'

The Bookwatch

KAREN STOHR

On
Manners

NEW YORK AND LONDON

First published 2012
by Routledge
711 Third Avenue, New York, NY 10017

Simultaneously published in the UK
by Routledge
2 Park Square, Milton Park, Abingdon, Oxon OX14 4RN

Routledge is an imprint of the Taylor & Francis Group, an informa business

Library of Congress Cataloging in Publication Data
Stohr, Karen.
  On manners/Karen Stohr.—1st ed.
  p. cm.—(Thinking in action)
  1. Etiquette. 2. Conduct of life. 3. Ethics. I. Title.
  BJ1838.S76 2011
  395—dc23   2011019899

ISBN: 978-0-415-87537-0 (hbk)
ISBN: 978-0-415-87538-7 (pbk)
ISBN: 978-0-203-85980-3 (ebk)

Typeset in Joanna and DIN
by Florence Production Ltd, Stoodleigh, Devon

Printed and bound in the United States of America on acid-free paper
by Edwards Brothers, Inc.

For my parents,
who taught me to care about
both morality and manners

Acknowledgments

Not much in academia gets accomplished without practical assistance, which I was fortunate enough to have during the writing of this book. I am grateful to Georgetown University for sabbatical leave and for providing fledgling faculty authors with moral support and good advice. My writing group, led by Carole Sargent, kept me on track and motivated during crucial points. I am indebted to Andy Beck and Emilie Littlehales at Routledge, and special thanks are due to Peter Johnson and a second, anonymous reviewer for Routledge for their extremely helpful comments on this manuscript.

I have many reasons to be grateful for my colleagues in Georgetown's philosophy department, not the least of which is the presence of so many talented philosophers with a deep appreciation for the practical significance of ethics. I have especially benefited from the wisdom of Maggie Little, Alisa Carse, Mark Lance, Bill Blattner, Judy Lichtenberg, Rebecca Kukla, Bryce Huebner, James Mattingly, Wayne Davis, and Anne Walsh. I am also grateful to my undergraduate and graduate students at Georgetown for letting me try out many of these ideas on them before foisting them on unsuspecting readers. Finally, I am particularly indebted to Tom Beauchamp, whose help during this process has been supererogatory on many levels.

My philosophical debt to Tom Hill—teacher, mentor, and friend—is enormous. Tom's quiet way of living out Kantian ideals is largely responsible for my own philosophical interest in it. If I have succeeded in making Kantianism appealing, it is because

I have had the good fortune to observe what it looks like in practice.

Ralph Waldo Emerson once remarked that "it is the blessing of old friends that you can afford to be stupid with them." I have had the luxury of being stupid in front of many friends over the years. My love of all things Jane Austen and Judith Martin has been fostered and challenged in different ways by Trudy Conway, Rosalind Hursthouse, Andrew Mills, David Rehm, David Solomon, Reed Solomon, Christine Swanton, Valerie Tiberius, and Anne Tumlinson. I owe special debts of gratitude to Claire Horisk and Gaby Sakamoto, whose insights into the themes in this book have proved invaluable. I particularly hope that the book reflects the wit and wisdom of Wendy Nankas and Lauren Fleming, two friends and fellow philosophers whose lives ended much too soon.

I am grateful beyond measure to my parents, Carolyn and Dick Stohr, to whom this book is dedicated. Aristotle claims that when it comes to moral character, upbringing is everything. If the wise advice of an expert in ethics or etiquette rings true in my ears, it is because of them. My parents also gave me the priceless gift of siblings who have grown into friends. My two sisters, Peggy and Kathy Stohr, have long served as a sounding board on problems great and small, and my brother, Greg Stohr, gave me much needed advice and encouragement in the writing of this book.

My husband, Bob Nonnenkamp, deserves his own paragraph. He has become better versed in Immanuel Kant and Emily Post than any other computer engineer on earth, and I love him all the more for it. I am especially grateful for the eight magic words that he said over and over again while I was working on this book: "I'll take care of that. You go write." No Austen heroine could be luckier in marriage than I have been.

And finally, I am grateful to Julia and Kate Nonnenkamp, who give joy to my days and meaning to my work. The major shock of having children is the realization that one has to raise them and that this involves teaching them things that are both useful and true. I hope that my daughters will grow up knowing which fork to use but also understanding how much more there is to having good manners. This book is largely a labor of love for them.

One

The fabric of society is very complex, George.[1]

Jerry Seinfeld

In an episode of the hit television sitcom *Seinfeld*, the socially inept George Costanza starts an argument with Elaine and Jerry about their plan to bring a gift to their friends' dinner party.[2] George begins by questioning the need to bring anything at all, and then makes a case for taking Pepsi and Ring Dings instead of wine and chocolate babka, as Elaine proposes. Elaine and Jerry insist that they have to bring something, but that it most definitely can't be Pepsi and Ring Dings.

Although Elaine and Jerry may be correct in their judgment about what counts as proper etiquette for a dinner guest, they struggle to come up with a response when George challenges them about the basis for that judgment. When George wonders why they can't show up empty-handed, Elaine just says that it is rude. When he goes on to ask what's wrong with bringing Pepsi instead of wine, Elaine's response consists of a glare and the remark that they are adults.

George acquiesces, but he clearly isn't satisfied. He argues that the other dinner guests would probably prefer Pepsi and Ring Dings to wine and babka. Strengthening his point is the fact that acquiring wine and chocolate babka proves to be a hugely difficult and time-consuming undertaking. By the time they get to the dinner party, it is late and they are too tired and grumpy to attend the party. When the hostess answers the door, they shove the wine and babka at her and go home. In the end we may find ourselves sympathizing with George's skepticism about the value of following this particular rule of etiquette. Maybe it really *would* have been better had they showed up with Ring Dings instead of babka, or even with nothing at all.

Seinfeld has often been described as a "show about nothing." There is a sense in which this is true; the series practically never grapples with any serious moral or political issues. And yet, there is also a sense in which it is not true that *Seinfeld* is about nothing. Rather, it is about many individually small problems that collectively take up a large percentage of our time and mental energy. Part of the genius of *Seinfeld* is its ability to highlight the pervasive ways in which social conventions and etiquette rules structure our day-to-day lives and also the way it calls into question the value of abiding by those conventions and rules.

Consider how many unwritten rules govern an ordinary and comparatively simple activity, like buying a drink at a busy Starbucks. There are conventions about standing in line, deciding what to order in advance of one's turn, moving out of the way of other customers while waiting for one's caramel macchiato, making room for people at the sugar and cream station, not taking up an excessively large table, not taking up any table for too long a time, and cleaning up after oneself upon leaving.

Some of these rules, like the rule that one should stand in line to order a drink, are both straightforward and widely accepted in American culture. Everyone knows what it means to stand in a line, and just about everyone does it. Rules about how much table space one can occupy and for how long, on the other hand, are much less clear. I may think that one person should never take up a four-person table, but you may think that you should be free to spread out your things in any unoccupied space. We might also disagree about whether it's rude for me to keep sitting at a table long after I've finished my coffee while newly arrived customers are waiting for a seat to open up. The rules that govern behavior in my local Starbucks could be different than they are, and probably are different in other Starbucks locations around the world. But just about any place we go, *some* customs and conventions are operating and many of us feel ourselves bound to act in accordance with them, though without always being sure why.

Humans are not the only animals who adhere to and enforce social conventions in groups. Anyone with a dog is bound to have noticed the elaborate system of body language and vocalizations that dogs use to establish their social positions and communicate with other dogs. But humans, unlike dogs, also have the capacity to raise questions about the purpose, significance, and social value of the conventions we're using. Like George, we can wonder whether the existing rules of etiquette are worth following, or whether they should be jettisoned in favor of new rules or even abandoned altogether. We can ask whether the social customs and conventions by which we live make our collective lives better, or whether they do more harm than good, perhaps by causing unneeded trouble (like the quest for chocolate babka does) or more sinisterly, by encouraging hypocrisy or enforcing hierarchies based on social class.

This book is an exploration of the theoretical basis of the rules and conventions of social life. What's the point of etiquette and what reason, if any, do we have to follow its dictates? Who has the authority to declare what counts as polite behavior and why should any of us pay attention? Does having good manners make me a better person? Does it improve my life in any way, or the lives of those around me? Is it *important*?

My claim in this book is that good manners are indeed important, that politeness does have a point. More specifically, it has a moral point.[3] I will make the case that rules of polite behavior are justified by their basis in commonly held moral principles and ideals, and that they play an essential role in enabling us to act on those principles and ideals. Social conventions help us communicate and act upon shared moral aims. They serve as vehicles through which we express important moral values like respect and consideration for the needs, ideas, and opinions of others.

This, of course, makes the practice of manners into a very lofty enterprise, which may seem peculiar to those who think of it primarily in terms of the proper use of forks at formal dinners. As will become clearer later in this chapter and in the next, I do not think polite behavior is all, or even mostly about forks. Making the connection between morality and manners requires rethinking and expanding our understanding of what it means to have good manners in the first place. George Costanza isn't exactly a model of politeness, but neither are Elaine and Jerry, who, despite their professed concern for rules about dinner parties, end up behaving quite badly in their single-minded quest for chocolate babka. On my account, good manners go hand in hand with good moral character. Virtuous people not only refrain from murdering, slandering, and stealing, but they also refrain from acting in self-important and obnoxious ways in bakeries. To put it differently, we might say that polite behavior is an extension of morality into small corners of our lives.

My behavior in Starbucks reveals quite a lot of information about my moral character and how I think about myself in relation to other people. If I cut to the front of the line, I am being arrogant, implying that my time is more important than anyone else's time. If I monopolize a large table during a busy time of day, I show that I am too self-absorbed to notice or care about what other people might need or want. By contrast, if I am willing to wait my turn, speak politely to other customers and the staff, and make a point of not taking up more than my own fair share of space, I indicate that I regard others as deserving the same kind of consideration that I think I warrant.

Certainly cutting to the front of a line in Starbucks is not a major moral offense. But it doesn't follow that rules about standing in line are unimportant from a moral standpoint. Indeed, American etiquette writer Judith Martin, better known as Miss Manners, claims that the rules of etiquette, far from being trivial, are essential to society itself:

> Trivial? Compared to what? World hunger? Yes, the little customs of society are less important than that. So is just about anything else. It is only once people are able to manage physical survival that manners become crucial. Then tradition is what gives a society meaning and the rules by which it lives are what make it work. We call that civilization.[4]

Martin's claim about the relationship between good manners and a functioning civilization may seem melodramatic. But the idea that some degree of civility is essential to any sort of shared public life is hardly new. Plenty of philosophers and political theorists—past and present—have made that case.[5] Moreover, for those who believe that contemporary American society is marked by declining standards of politeness, Martin's concerns about civilization seem quite real. Attack ads in political campaigns, rude and unnecessarily inflammatory protests, road rage that quickly escalates into violence— all these things give the impression that American society is just barely containing itself, and sometimes not even managing that.

It's tempting to romanticize various times in the past as having been more civil, more polite, and more gracious than current American culture seems to be. But it's not clear that there was ever a golden age in history in which people were better-mannered than we are now. Anyway, even if it's true that Americans are ruder to each other than we ever have been before, at least we are now comparatively egalitarian in our rudeness. These days we seem to accept that everyone is equally deserving of incivility, regardless of race, sex, or creed. From a moral standpoint, that is undoubtedly an improvement over the racist and sexist codes of manners from the past. Still, a community in which people routinely behave rudely to each other in the local Starbucks is probably not a community in which most of us want to live.

The question of why we should bother to be polite bears considerable resemblance to a longstanding question in moral philosophy about why we should bother to be moral. What does it matter whether I follow the rules of polite behavior or, for that matter, the rules of moral behavior? The seventeenth-century British philosopher Thomas Hobbes argued in his masterpiece, *Leviathan*, that in the absence of enforceable moral rules, human beings would be living in what he called the "state of nature." In the state of nature, everyone is out for himself or herself. The goal is to stay alive, and people in the state of nature will do whatever it takes to achieve that end. (Hobbes went further and argued that people have a *right* in the state of nature to do and take what's necessary to stay alive.) Any alliances or bonds formed in the state of nature are tenuous—they last only so long as it is to the advantage of each member of the alliance that they continue.

Hobbes thinks that life in the state of nature is unbearable, famously describing it as "solitary, poor, nasty, brutish, and short."[6] It is not a state in which any rational person would want to remain; indeed, Hobbes thinks that our own self-interest directs us to do what we can to get out of the state of nature. Each of us is better served, he argues, by giving up some of our natural right to do whatever we want so as to be free from the dangers imposed on us by the exercise of equivalent rights by others. In other words, it makes sense for me to give up my freedom to take your property by force if I can be sure that you and everybody else will leave my property alone. Hobbes argued that this state of civil society in which people sacrifice some freedoms for greater security against harm, makes us all better off.[7]

Civil society as Hobbes understood it can only exist if there is someone capable of enforcing the rules. In *Leviathan*, Hobbes calls this person (who doesn't actually have to be a person) the sovereign. Hobbes's sovereign is extremely powerful, something that Hobbes thought necessary for the maintenance of any kind of moral community. If the sovereign isn't capable of coercing people into following the rules, then society just reverts back to the state of nature. People agree to hand over many of their natural rights to the sovereign in exchange for assurance that other people are doing the same. It would be like a group of armed people agreeing that everyone should hand over their guns to a particular individual. That individual becomes extremely powerful, but everyone else becomes equally defenseless. Hobbes thinks that this is an improvement over a situation in which everyone is armed. In his version of civil society, I have to watch out for the sovereign, but at least I no longer have to worry about being killed by the person sitting next to me.

In a Hobbesian world, we do have reason to follow the rules of morality, but crucially, it is a self-interested reason. Hobbes set up his theory this way because he believed that as a matter of human psychology, we are only motivated by what's in our own self interest. We could probably construct a decent Hobbesian argument for good manners based on self-interest alone. We are all better off if we are willing to stand in line in Starbucks because eventually we will all get our coffee and no one will end up getting poked in the eye by a coffee stirrer. It is a system that benefits me overall, and on a Hobbesian-style view of manners, that gives me reason to participate in it.

The idea that we should be polite primarily because it will bring us individual rewards is often associated with one of history's most famous proponents of good manners, the 4th Earl of Chesterfield. In the eighteenth century, Lord Chesterfield wrote a series of letters to his illegitimate son, whose education he was overseeing. The letters exhort the teenaged Philip to cultivate good manners and they give him advice about how a young man in his circumstances should comport himself across a variety of social circumstances. Indeed, the letters make clear that Chesterfield thought that good manners would be exceedingly important to Philip's success in life, perhaps as important as any other aspect of his education. The letters caused controversy when they were published because people interpreted Chesterfield as suggesting that good manners are important only insofar as they serve to help a person get ahead. Samuel Johnson, who was perhaps Chesterfield's harshest critic, famously said of Chesterfield's letters that "they teach the morals of a whore, and the manners of a dancing master."[8]

Johnson's attack on Chesterfield is clever, but probably not entirely fair. As we will see later in this chapter, Chesterfield was quite concerned with the development of Philip's moral character as well. Nevertheless, the general worry motivating Johnson's wisecrack is a legitimate one. If the only point of cultivating good manners is that it will further my own reputation and interests in the world, that doesn't seem terribly satisfying. Moreover, if the only reasons that I have to behave politely are self-interested ones, what happens in circumstances where my self-interest is not served by being polite?

In Hobbesian civil society, violations of moral rules are punished by the sovereign. This means that it's never in my self-interest to violate the rules that the sovereign puts in place. Likewise in our society, when there are legal sanctions in place for bad behavior, I always have at least some reason not to engage in it if there's any chance I will be caught and punished. But of course it's not against the law to cut in line at Starbucks. There are no roving bands of etiquette police officers nabbing offenders and putting them behind bars.

If there are going to be any sanctions for rudeness, they will have to be enforced informally by fellow members of the community. In some circumstances, this works quite well. Suppose

I live in a small town where Starbucks is the only coffee shop. If I cut in line, I am likely offending people I will also see at the hardware store, church, gym, and PTA meetings. It's probably not worth it to me to jump to the front of the line if I will damage my social standing as a result, and be excluded or ignored at other events and activities that I care about.

Increasingly, however, this is not how many of our interactions with other people work. One fact about the contemporary age is that we spend more of our time being anonymous than ever before. If we live in big cities or heavily populated suburbs, we can cut people off in traffic on the highway knowing that we are highly unlikely ever to see those particular drivers again. Even if we did see them in Starbucks the next day, they probably wouldn't recognize us. The internet, of course, takes anonymity to an entirely new level. I can post obnoxious or inflammatory comments on blogs or websites without any real risk of having those comments traced back to me by anyone I know. (At worst, my IP address might get banned.) In other words, it has probably never been easier to get away with rude behavior than it is today. If Hobbes is right that our only reason to follow the rules is that we will suffer repercussions if we don't, then maybe contemporary society really is in danger of collapsing into a state of total rudeness.

But perhaps Hobbes isn't right. Perhaps there *are* reasons to be nice to each other that don't just come back to what's in each person's self-interest. In his famous work, *The Republic*, the ancient Greek philosopher Plato took up the question of whether we have reason to behave well even when we can get away with misbehavior. One of the characters in the dialogue, Glaucon, raises the problem by way of the fable of the Ring of Gyges. The ring has the power to turn its wearer invisible, thereby making it possible for the ring's owner to get away with anything that he or she attempts. Glaucon suggests that anyone who had the ring would act unjustly and that moreover, a person who had the ring but who didn't use it to its full advantage would be a fool.[9]

Plato's response to Glaucon's challenge is to argue, via the character of Socrates, that people who never constrain themselves, who follow their desires wherever they lead, end up being effectively enslaved by those desires. True, the person who possesses the Ring of Gyges can do whatever she wants whenever she wants, but, Plato argues, it's not an enviable way to live. The wearer of the ring may think that by doing whatever she wants, she is acting freely, but Plato claimed that this is an illusion of sorts. Such a person has no incentive to master her desires, and so she becomes mastered by them. (The character of Gollum from Tolkien's *Lord of the Rings* series exemplifies this perfectly; he is entirely enslaved and eventually destroyed by his desire for the ring and its powers.) According to Plato, true freedom and true happiness are possible only when people live according to reason, rather than following each desire wherever it might lead.

This idea that there is something liberating about good behavior will be picked up by Plato's intellectual descendant, the eighteenth-century Prussian philosopher Immanuel Kant, whom we will encounter often in this book. As we will see, Kant thinks it is possible to give an account of why we should behave ourselves that does *not* depend on contingent facts about what happens to be in our self-interest at the moment. In Kant's eyes, I have reason to stand in line in Starbucks even in circumstances when I could get away with cutting to the front without suffering any consequences. The reasons have to do with respecting both myself and other people as fellow members of a moral community, or, to use Kant's language, as fellow members of the kingdom of ends.

Let's see how this works. Kant held the view that to be a rational being is to have a certain kind of moral standing. He expressed this by saying that rational agents are ends in themselves, never to be used as a mere means to someone else's plans or projects.

(This is what is known as the "humanity formulation" of Kant's famous foundational moral principle, which he called the "categorical imperative.") Kant explained what it means to be an end by arguing that rational beings have dignity and unconditional value. If I have dignity, that means that my value is incommensurable; it cannot be compared or traded off against the value of anything else. If I have unconditional value, that means that I have value that does not depend on anyone's attitudes about me or opinions about my worth.

Objects, by contrast, have only price and conditional value. Ballpoint pens and telephones can legitimately be bought and sold, and their value can be determined in terms of money. They are also conditionally valuable, meaning that they are valuable only so long as someone finds them useful or important.[10] If the pen belongs to me, I am free to dispose of it when I am through using it. I can also sell it on eBay for something I like better without thereby wronging the pen. Rational beings cannot legitimately be treated this way. On Kant's view, we deserve respect in virtue of our status as ends with dignity and unconditional value. Treating a person as an object is disrespectful because it fails to acknowledge that status.

This may all seem pretty obvious, which is actually how Kant intended it to seem. He believed that he was simply articulating, albeit in a very complex way, the ordinary moral intuitions of good, reflective people. As we will see in later chapters, this obvious-sounding principle turns out to have some rather startling implications. But for now, its obviousness is an advantage.

Importantly, Kant thought that I have the same obligation to treat myself with respect as I have to treat other people with respect. I even have a duty of self-respect to insist that others treat me as an end. If I let other people walk all over me, I fail to treat myself as having the same moral status as they do. In fact, Kant believed that a person who lacks self-respect is not fully able to respect other people as ends. This is because my understanding of what it is for other people to have that kind of moral status stems from my understanding of my own moral status. It's through thinking about myself and the kind of consideration that I think I warrant that enables me to see why other people warrant the same consideration.

Let's return to the example of cutting in line, which will help make this clear. The point of a line, of course, is to ensure that people are treated according to a fair procedure, which in this case is "first come, first served." When I join a line, I expect that this procedure will be followed. If someone cuts in front of me, he is certainly violating a rule of etiquette. But with the resources of Kant's humanity formulation, we can say something more.

Lines are one way of demonstrating a commitment to the equal standing of other people. The person who cuts in line is expressing a disregard for that commitment. Either he doesn't think that he needs to take other people into account at all, or else he thinks that there is something that justifies his being served ahead of other people. Kant's humanity formulation can readily show what's wrong with this way of thinking. The line-cutter is right to think that his needs and plans deserve consideration, but he is mistaken to think that they deserve *greater* consideration than the needs and plans of other people just in virtue of being his own. In fact, Kant believed that this is actually an irrational way of thinking, as well as immoral.

The success of the line-cutter's action depends on other people remaining in line. If everyone acted as he did, we would have not a line but a mob. Rational reflection shows that the line-cutter is attempting to make an exception of himself, wanting everyone else to abide by a rule while he ignores it. The line-cutter's mistake is in thinking that this can be justified by an appeal to his special importance. But his status is the same as everyone else's— whatever reasons he has to stay in line or cut the line are also reasons for everyone else to do the same. No doubt, his afternoon plans are important to him, but from the standpoint of rationality, they are no more important than the afternoon plans of anyone else. He is an equal member of the community of rational agents, but he is not superior to anyone in it, nor can his belief that he is superior withstand rational scrutiny.

Of course there can be good reasons for cutting in line. If you are on the verge of discovering a cure for cancer and need to get back to your lab before the cells divide again, the rest of us might well be willing to let you ahead of us. The crucial feature here, though, is that the reason offered is a reason that the rest of us can accept. Ambulances are permitted to cut to the front of the line of cars because each of us can readily see that if it were me or my loved one in the ambulance, I'd want the ambulance to get to the hospital faster. Emergencies are situations that generate what everyone recognizes to be good reasons why a particular person's needs or plans should be given priority. So it's not that there can never be justification for jumping to the front of the line, nor does line-cutting always convey the attitude that the line-cutter is somehow superior to other people. But very often it does. When that is the case, Kant's theory can help us see the connection between the rude act of cutting in line and the deeper moral problem with the line-cutter's attitude about himself in relationship to others. Jumping in line is not simply a violation of etiquette; it raises moral concerns as well. And those moral concerns are the basis for its rudeness.

In defending the importance of manners in this book, I will opt for a route more like the Kantian one rather than the Hobbesian one. Although it is reasonable to suppose that adhering to the conventions of etiquette generally does serve my own interest, this is not the only reason I have to adhere to them. Over the course of this book, I will show that the reasons that we have for being moral are also reasons for being polite. More specifically, I will argue that behaving politely is a *way* of behaving morally. Manners, we might say, are the outward expression of moral character.

In contemporary society, we are not accustomed to thinking of manners and morals as being related. In fact, it is often presumed that we can draw a sharp distinction between the concerns of morality and the concerns of manners. For one thing, our experience of the world would seem to indicate that morality and manners can come apart. Most of us know people with excellent manners and rotten characters, and likewise people with sterling moral qualities and cringe-worthy manners.

Second, we tend to view moral questions as serious issues that ought to concern everyone. Questions of etiquette, by contrast, are thought to be comparatively frivolous, something mostly of concern to people getting married or hosting formal dinner parties.[11] In libraries and bookstores, etiquette books are never located in the same section as books in moral philosophy. Although just about every major newspaper carries etiquette and other behavior advice columns, they are usually relegated to the "style" section, alongside horoscopes, comics, and articles about New York Fashion Week. These practices reinforce the idea that manners are about the external trappings of life, not its vital substance.

This is in part, I think, because for many people what comes to mind when they think about etiquette is a set of rules about things like what fork to use during the salad course, or what color of shoes to wear after Labor Day, or how to address a social invitation to a pair of veterinarians. It's true that there are rules about such things, but it's also obviously the case that those rules are conventional, tied to a particular time and place, and not terribly important in the fact of pressing concerns like hunger, disease, terrorism, and global warming. It is hard to see how the specifics of table settings and seasonal footwear could possibly have any moral implications. Likewise, when confronted with major moral questions, we do not generally focus on issues of proper form. Probably it is possible to murder someone more or less politely, but the moral gravity of the act means that considerations of rudeness largely fall by the wayside. At the extremes, the concerns of morality seem quite distant from the concerns of manners.

And yet, it does not take much reflection to recognize that there is a great deal of space in the middle. If I am at a cocktail party and the person with whom I am speaking tells a racist joke, do I have a moral problem on my hands or an etiquette problem? Or both? In fact, many of our everyday practical problems involve issues of both morality and manners, and there is no very good way to draw a distinction between them. Actual advice columns reflect the blurred boundary between etiquette and ethics. Although technically Judith Martin is an etiquette columnist and Randy Cohen of the *New York Times* is an ethics columnist, there is considerable overlap in the kinds of questions posed to them.

This presumption that etiquette is an entirely separate subject from ethics is prevalent in moral philosophy as well. Only very rarely do contemporary philosophers take seriously the idea that etiquette is a serious topic, worthy of philosophical reflection in its own right.[12] In philosophy journal articles, if the rules of etiquette are brought up at all, it is usually for the purposes of drawing a contrast with moral rules. Interestingly, though, this trivialization of etiquette is a fairly new phenomenon in philosophy. The current relegation of manners to the philosophical back burner is actually an historical anomaly.

Some of the most famous moral philosophers in history took questions of manners quite seriously and discussed them alongside what we tend to think of as more pressing moral issues. Great thinkers like Aristotle, Kant, and David Hume wrote about topics that are now mostly the subject of letters to advice columnists. (Thus Kant, who wrote some of the most difficult, abstract philosophical texts in existence, also voiced opinions about the ideal number of guests at a dinner party and topics of conversation to be avoided at the table.) Writers, politicians, and public intellectuals, including widely beloved authors like Jane

situation. As Elizabeth says in reference to Darcy and Wickham, "There certainly was some great mismanagement in the education of those two young men. One has got all the goodness, and the other all the appearance of it."[15] Darcy has the goodness, but not the appearance, whereas Wickham has the appearance of goodness without the actual goodness to back it up. Of course Austen prizes actual goodness over the appearance of goodness, which is why Darcy is the hero of *Pride and Prejudice*, not Wickham. Even so, it's clear that Austen thinks a good man like Darcy is improved when he acquires the manners to match his character.

In this book, I am going to defend this old-fashioned idea that good moral character is enhanced and completed by good manners. I will argue that it is an idea as applicable today as it was in Austen's time, although a twenty-first-century Elizabeth Bennet would probably be criticizing Darcy's behavior on Facebook rather than his behavior at a ball. I will also argue that we can glean quite a lot of insight about how to navigate contemporary social life by reflecting on the wisdom produced by highly regarded philosophers of the past. As we'll see, Kant's ethical theory produces all kinds of conclusions of practical value for anyone trying to sort out the nuances of social behavior, including self-presentation, polite lies, gift-giving, and relationships with neighbors. Aristotle can help us understand the relationship between general etiquette rules and their application to specific situations, as well as the role of etiquette experts in helping us bridge that gap. If, while watching HGTV or reading *Apartment Therapy*, we find ourselves wondering about what makes certain physical spaces welcoming and hospitable and what that reflects about their owners, a look at David Hume's theory about taste (which has echoes in Emily Post and Martha Stewart) will help.

Thus far, I have made the claim that good manners are much more closely intertwined with good character than either contemporary culture or contemporary moral philosophy acknowledges. Thinking about manners as part of morality itself helps illuminate the kinds of reasons that we have to be polite, and also show why those reasons aren't simply based in self-interest. If Jerry and Elaine were a bit more reflective, or had read a bit more philosophy, they probably would have been able to give George a better answer to his question about why wine and babka are preferable to Pepsi and Ring Dings.

But the general claim that manners are connected to moral principles is not by itself sufficient to respond to George's challenge. After all, George is not arguing that the party hosts don't warrant respect and consideration. Rather, he is disputing the idea that following this very specific etiquette convention, at least as it is proclaimed by Elaine, is somehow essential to showing respect and consideration for them. On his view, picking up Pepsi and Ring Dings at the corner store would serve that purpose just as well or better. In order to answer George, it will be necessary to say more about the relationship between moral principles and rules of etiquette that are obviously tied to local conventions and customs. That will be my project in the next chapter.

The Link Between Morality and Manners

Two

Nothing so needs reforming as other people's habits.[1]

Mark Twain

In the introductory chapter, I argued that there is no sharp distinction between the concerns of morality and the concerns of manners. Having good manners is, I suggested, part of what it means to have a good moral character. But there are some obstacles to thinking this way. While we tend to believe that moral rules and principles express absolute, universal norms, etiquette rules are clearly conventional, varying across time and place. Because of this, it seems as though etiquette rules just don't carry the same kind of authority as moral rules. This is the point that George is pushing in the *Seinfeld* episode discussed in the last chapter. He is not arguing with Elaine and Jerry about what the existing convention is; rather, he is challenging its basis and suggesting that it can and should be ignored or at least amended.

I claimed in the last chapter that the convention of waiting in line is a morally significant one in American culture. What makes cutting in line rude in American society is that it expresses the attitude that the line-cutter's needs and plans are more important than anyone else's, and that this is disrespectful to the other people in line. But of course, not all societies have such strong views about line formation; in some places, people rarely form lines at all and cutting to the front is not a big deal. Obviously we can't infer that people in those societies don't respect each other.

If etiquette conventions vary from culture to culture, how can they possibly be based in a universal moral principle like Kant's categorical imperative?

Kant himself distinguished between two types of imperatives: hypothetical and categorical. Imperatives, for Kant, are commands of one's own reason, not orders given by an external authority. They are commands that I give to myself, such as when I tell myself that I need to get more regular exercise. This is, as we know, a rather different phenomenon than being commanded to exercise by one's doctor or one's drill sergeant. When I tell myself to do something, it carries a different kind of authority, an internal one. Of course I can "disobey" myself by not exercising, but if I do that, I will be failing myself and not acting in accordance with my own best judgment about how I ought to behave. Kant believed that morality works something like this. It is a command that gets its authority for me from the fact that I, as a rational being, issue it to myself.

When I recognize that I am under an imperative, I acknowledge that I am rationally required to do something (or refrain from doing something). A hypothetical imperative is a conditional requirement. Its basic form is this: if you have X as your end, do Y. Whether Y is a requirement of reason depends on whether you have X as your end. For someone who doesn't care about X, Y has no rational force.

For example, let's suppose that I want to see a show tonight that is nearly sold out. If that's the case, there's something that I need to be doing; namely, buying tickets for it as soon as possible. In Kant's schema, the imperative, "If I want tickets for tonight's show, I should buy them now" is a hypothetical imperative. If I don't want tickets to the show, I have no reason to buy any now. But if I do want tickets to the show, then I have two rational options available to me. I can either buy the tickets now or I can change my mind about seeing tonight's show. Either way makes sense from the point of view of rationality. What is irrational is continuing to want to see the show, but failing to buy tickets.

Kant argued that the supreme principle of morality is a categorical imperative, not a hypothetical one. This means that it has the simpler form, "Do Y." The conditional part of the imperative is absent because Kant believed that we are all already rationally committed to the end of being a morally good person. Once I realize what it means for me to have dignity and hence, to be worthy of respectful treatment, I must (if I am to be consistent) recognize the dignity and respect-worthiness of others. This commits me to behaving morally, Kant thought. So a categorical imperative, unlike a hypothetical imperative, leaves me with only one rational option, which is to do what it commands. Unlike the end of wanting to see a show, the end of acting morally is not one that I can rationally give up. To be immoral, for Kant, is to be irrational.

Most people take for granted that the commands of etiquette are, at best, hypothetical imperatives.[2] If one cares about being polite, one should act according to the dictates of etiquette. But if etiquette commands are hypothetical, then the end of being polite is optional, and not a rational requirement. On this view, the rules of etiquette are like the rules of a game. You're bound by the rules of a game so long as you're playing, but you're not obligated to play. And if you are not playing the game, the rules have no authority over you. If I am yelling "Marco," I cannot complain that you are not yelling "Polo" if you haven't agreed to play Marco Polo with me.

As is probably obvious by now, I do not think that the rules of etiquette are merely hypothetical imperatives. My claim is that they are binding on me whether or not I have it as my end to be polite. "I don't care about being polite" is no better a defense against cutting in line than "I don't care about being moral" is against swiping someone's purse. But in order to make this claim persuasive, I need to say more about the relationship between universal moral principles and conventional rules of etiquette.

The best way to make this case, I think, is to employ a distinction between the principles of manners and the rules of etiquette drawn by Judith Martin in her book, *A Citizen's Guide to Civility*:

> Miss Manners uses the word "manners" to refer to the principles underlying any system of etiquette, and "etiquette" to refer to the particular rules used to express these principles. . . . Because etiquette rules are fashioned to pertain to a particular time and social setting, they are subject to development and change. However, the principles of manners from which they derive their authority remain constant and universal. Even directly contradictory rules of etiquette prevailing in different societies at the same time, or at different times in the same society, may derive their authority from the same principle of manners.[3]

This connection between specific, highly conventional rules of etiquette and broader, universal principles of manners will prove to be very important in this book. In a nutshell, I will argue that the principles of manners are moral principles, and specific rules of etiquette get their authority from their relationship to those moral principles. Acting in accordance with the rules of polite behavior operative in a given society is a way of acting on more universal moral concerns.

Martin's definition acknowledges the conventionality of rules about standing in line and using proper table manners. Taken by themselves, the rules are not especially important, and we could readily imagine living in a world in which these rules did not apply. But what gives the particular rules that happen to be in place in our society their authority is that they enable us to put principles of manners into practice in the culture in which we happen to live. They are binding insofar as they are the established vehicle through which we express the important moral aims and goals reflected in the principles of manners. (This is not to say that all existing rules of etiquette are binding on us. I will return to this issue later in the chapter.)

Consider the rules of etiquette governing proper attire. Obviously, specific rules about what clothing is appropriate to wear in what circumstances are rules of etiquette and, as such, highly conventional. What is not conventional, however, is the fact that wearing appropriate clothing is an important way of expressing respect for other people and the occasions they are celebrating. The idea that one should show respect for other people is a principle of manners; wearing certain clothing is one way of accomplishing it. The reason why it is ordinarily an etiquette violation to wear shorts and flip-flops to an American funeral is that shorts and flip-flops convey a relaxed, carefree attitude at odds with the solemnity and gravity appropriate to a funeral. One is supposed to take death seriously, and wearing serious clothes to a funeral is a way to show respect for the deceased and one's fellow mourners. Our definition of serious clothes is culturally specific, but insofar as it is the operative definition, we are bound by it.[4]

As Martin points out, the rules of etiquette found in different cultures or different time periods can conflict with each other, while still being justified by a single principle of manners. For instance, she claims that it is a universal principle of manners that "guests must show respect for their hosts, and hosts must show honor to their guests."[5] But how this principle translates into particular actions varies from culture to culture. For instance, in Japan, a respectful guest removes his shoes; in some parts of the United States, automatically removing one's shoes would be disrespectful. The principle of respect underlying the two rules essentially the same; it is just that different cultures have different conventions for showing respect to one's host.

Martin's position is that while the rules of etiquette are conventional and culturally specific, the underlying principles of manners are not. On my account, this is because what she calls the principles of manners are moral principles. Now of course, some people hold the view that moral principles are just as conventional as etiquette rules. This view, however, is rather unpopular within moral philosophy. Indeed, most philosophers in history have agreed that there is something universal about morality, even if they disagree about what morality is and what makes it universal.

As we have seen, Kant believes that the categorical imperative, his supreme moral principle, is binding on all rational agents. It is a command of rationality; we act irrationally when we act immorally. Kant spelled out four (or perhaps three or five, depending on how we count) formulations of the categorical imperative, believing that they were equivalent. In the last chapter's example about line-jumping, I employed what is known as the humanity formulation, which tells us that we should always treat rational beings, ourselves and others, as ends in themselves, with dignity and unconditional value. I suggested that this principle can be used to make sense of just what it is about cutting in line that is so offensive in a culture that takes lines seriously.

I will employ the humanity formulation of the categorical imperative quite a bit in this book, since I think that it is an excellent way to make sense of principles of manners like "show respect" and "be considerate of other people." There are, however, other ways of thinking about the moral principles underlying the specific conventions of polite behavior. As we will see in the next chapter, twentieth-century etiquette expert Emily Post justifies the rules of etiquette and good taste in terms of their utility and, to a lesser extent, their overall pleasingness. She would have found considerable philosophical support for this view in the theory of the eighteenth-century British philosopher David Hume.

Hume, a well-traveled and talented observer of human behavior, recognized that different cultures employ very different conventions of manners:

Many of the forms of breeding are arbitrary and casual: But the thing expressed by them is still the same. A Spaniard goes out of his own house before his guest, to signify that he leaves him master of all. In other countries, the landlord walks out last, as a common mark of deference and regard.[6]

But the various conventions are grounded in something common, namely, their overall role in fostering a pleasant social life. Hume believed that we evaluate character traits and the behavior that emanates from them in terms of the utility and agreeableness of those traits. Traits that are useful or agreeable, whether to ourselves or others, are virtues. Politeness, cheerfulness, and an overall sense of decorum are, according to Hume, agreeable in themselves and useful for sustaining social harmony. The specific conventions that enable us to express those traits may vary, but the value of the traits themselves does not.

There are still other philosophical supports for the idea that the rules of etiquette have moral significance. Adherents of a moral theory known as utilitarianism believe that right actions are those that maximize happiness, meaning that they bring about the best consequences for all those affected by the action.[7] Many rules of etiquette, particularly those governing our movement in public, are aimed at allowing us to travel efficiently through our day. It is a convention of subway travel that people wanting to board a subway car at a stop should wait until people leaving the car have gotten off. This is not because the people getting off the car are more important than the people getting on, but because the convention provides an efficient way for a subway to exchange passengers in a short period of time. Rules of etiquette can benefit everyone by improving efficiency and reducing the likelihood of conflict.

Yet another way of grounding the value of etiquette can be found in the theory of the ancient Greek philosopher Aristotle. Aristotle, like Hume, was primarily interested in character traits, but he was also quite interested in how those character traits issue in concrete actions. In the next chapter, I will devote a great deal of space to Aristotle's understanding of virtue, particularly the virtue that he called *phronesis*, or practical wisdom. Practical wisdom, I will argue, is an essential part of expertise in both morality and manners. It takes practical wisdom to have good manners because behaving politely is far more complicated than simply following a list of etiquette rules in a book somewhere.

Taken by themselves, these moral theories are deeply incompatible in very important ways. I am mostly going to ignore those incompatibilities, on the grounds that seeing what makes philosophical theories distinct from each other is not particularly important to my project here. I am more interested in showing how moral theories can be used both to shed light on the moral basis of manners itself and to generate and justify particular rules of etiquette. I will be relying most heavily on Kant's account of morality, but other approaches will play important supporting roles in different chapters.

Let me return to the distinction between the principles of manners, understood as moral principles, and the conventional rules of etiquette. How is it that the rules of etiquette express or further the moral ideals and aims expressed in the principles of manners? I suggest that it is largely in virtue of their ability to serve as vehicles of communication and expression. My choice of clothing for a funeral and my behavior at a dinner party in someone's home are actions that send a message to other people. The fact that etiquette conventions function as communication devices is what makes it possible to use them to further moral aims.

Take, for instance, the very simple and widespread etiquette convention of attaching the word "please" to a request. Contemporary philosopher Sarah Buss has argued that the word "please" is serving to acknowledge the other person as something like a Kantian end.[8] One function of "please" in conversation is to mark something as a request rather than a command or demand. In social life, it is rare for anyone to have the authority to command another adult to do something. The presumption is that the person being asked to pass the salt has the right to decline. (This doesn't mean that it would be kind or charitable to decline. It's possible to be a jerk while exercising one's legitimate rights.) The word "please" acknowledges this fact. To put it in Kantian terms, the word "please" is a public recognition of the other person's status as a rational being, an end in herself. Even when attached to something that's genuinely a command, "please" still serves to acknowledge the other person as an independent agent. This is how the use of the word communicates respect. It expresses my recognition of the fact that the other person is on an equal footing with me, and that I am not authorized to command or direct her behavior.

Of course, we sometimes do say "please" to people even when we are genuinely in a position to give them commands. Parents frequently add "please" when they tell their children to go to bed or stop arguing. In the workplace, managers often do the same thing when giving directions to people who report to them. Issuing orders that are phrased like requests might seem deceptive. "Please get this report to me by 5:00" is not really a request when it comes from one's boss. And yet, the fact that Mildred is Elmer's boss doesn't mean that there isn't some sense in which Mildred and Elmer remain on an equal footing. Mildred does have the authority to give Elmer commands in the workplace, but she can't legitimately command all aspects of his behavior in the office, and she certainly cannot command him to do things outside the workplace. She cannot, for instance, order him to make his bed in the morning, Elmer's moral status doesn't change just because Mildred is his boss; she still has to respect him as an end in Kant's sense, even when she gives him orders. Attaching "please" to her demand that he finish the report by 5:00 is one way of acknowledging this. (So is refraining from demeaning him or making unreasonable demands about his attire and behavior at work.)

The rule that one must say "please" when making a request is certainly conventional. We might have chosen a different word. As Buss points out, we could accomplish the same end by saying "Pass the salt, you are worthy of respect" instead of "Pass the salt, please." But since our existing convention for making standard requests involves the word "please," that gives all of us reason to abide by that convention, rather than making up our own. The word "please" is an agreed-upon device for showing respect. Showing respect is a moral requirement, and insofar as saying "please" is the established way of communicating that respect, it is a morally important thing to do.[9]

Along similar lines, the rudeness of cutting in line is based in the fact that in American culture, standing in a line is also a way of conveying respect. When I join a line by going to the end of it, I signal to the other people waiting that I intend to abide by the established conventions regarding lines. My expressed willingness to adhere to the convention communicates my belief that I stand on an equal footing with them, that I don't regard my needs and priorities as more important than theirs just because they happen to be mine. True, they may not know whether I am doing this because I really do believe them to be my moral equals or because I am afraid of the social disapproval I will face if I cut the line. Still, by standing in line, I am publicly accepting that the convention has authority for me, that it binds me in the same way that it binds everyone else. I present myself to the other people as one among equals.

By contrast, if I jump to the front of the line, I convey the attitude that I do not take myself to be bound by the same rules as everyone else. Now if I happen to be bleeding profusely, people may infer that my line-cutting is a result of pain or desperation, not a superiority complex. But if I have no evident reason for cutting, one that others can see and accept, they will infer that I think I am better or more important than them. And they are right to find that offensive and disrespectful.

Lines do not, of course, play the same communicative role in every culture or subculture. In a community that does not interpret cutting in line as an expression of disrespect, the act of cutting in line might well be morally innocuous. The rudeness of cutting in line depends on what conventions happen to be operating in a given setting and what the willingness or unwillingness to abide by those conventions expresses to other people. It is both about what I intend to communicate and also what message my audience receives.

If etiquette rules are to play the communicative function I have assigned to them, then they must be based on established conventions. Otherwise, there is no way for them to succeed in transmitting the relevant information. Rules of etiquette, like the rules of traffic, depend on widespread agreement about both their content and the degree to which they bind us. Although the meaning of a stop sign is highly conventional, I cannot change its meaning at will and certainly not by myself. Stop signs command me to stop, regardless of whether I want to stop or think it necessary to stop. Of course ignoring traffic rules is a threat to human welfare, which is why we think it appropriate to back them up with legal sanctions and coerce people into following them. Etiquette rules are not ordinarily backed up with legal sanctions, but it doesn't follow that they are not binding or that any one individual has the power to change them. If social customs serve as the vehicles through which we communicate moral attitudes to others, we cannot single-handedly change the language through which those attitudes are spoken.

Once we understand the communicative function of social conventions, we can see why they simultaneously provide us with a very compelling reason to adhere to them and also permission to override, change, or ignore them on occasions where the convention isn't necessary to fulfill the moral aim. If I say to a stranger at a wedding dinner, "Pass the salt, you idiot," I am obviously behaving rudely. I must say "please" in this context because it is the established way to convey respect in the context of making a request, and I have to express my respect in a way that I can be reasonably sure he will understand. But I can say, "Pass the salt, you idiot" to my brother without necessarily being rude if I am doing so affectionately and my brother understands "you idiot" to be a term of endearment and not an insult. Here it is the relationship that makes it possible to set aside the standard conventions. If my brother and I have a genuine understanding according to which such an expression counts as affectionate rather than disrespectful, then "please" may be unnecessary. But that is only because my brother and I are communicating through different conventions than the established ones. In general, the fewer alternative ways we have to communicate our respect to people, the more important standard social conventions become. It's one thing to bring Ring Dings to a dinner party hosted by a good friend; it's something else to bring them to a dinner party hosted by someone I barely know.

Critics of this view might be inclined to set aside the communication of respect as not especially important, or at least less important than other ways of respecting people. Respect for you requires both that I refrain from killing you and also that I make room when you get on the elevator. Certainly the requirement that I not kill you is the more pressing requirement of the two. But we should not dismiss the importance of communicated respect to our moral relationships with both friends and strangers.

In his famous "Letter from a Birmingham Jail," Martin Luther King Jr. spelled out a number of ways in which black people were being treated unequally and unjustly. Some of the actions that he listed are clear violations of moral principles, such as police brutality, church bombings, and the segregation of schools and public buildings. But in that masterfully crafted letter, King also made a point of mentioning the conventions by which African

Americans were standardly addressed at the time. He remarks that his wife and mother were never given "the respected title of 'Mrs.'" as they would have been had they been white.[10] King was surely right that this practice was deeply disrespectful of black women, and it is noteworthy that he thought it important enough to include it in his list of grievances, despite it being primarily a matter of etiquette.

Now it might be thought that King's point about the use of honorific titles actually poses an objection to the idea that the rules of etiquette are binding on us. After all, the convention at that time in most of the United States was not to use honorifics when addressing African Americans, to use first names only or to address adults by terms like "boy." People who followed that convention were, deliberately or not, communicating disrespect and contributing to the oppressive structures of racism. It was the people who bucked social convention and used the same titles for people regardless of race who were behaving in the most morally defensible way. Doesn't that undermine the claim that it's morally important to follow the rules of etiquette? Indeed, isn't this a situation in which we would be morally obligated not to follow existing conventions?

One of the advantages of distinguishing between principles of manners (which, remember, I'm interpreting as moral principles) and rules of etiquette is that it gives us a way to answer this objection. This is because on this account, the criterion for whether something is a legitimate rule of etiquette is not simply whether it is the convention actually in use, but whether it is consistent with the underlying principles of manners. It enables us to subject our conventions to critical scrutiny, and also to adapt and change them as our moral attitudes and principles evolve.

In the case of racist social conventions, it is clear that the problem is with the principle underlying the conventions of addressing people differently depending on their race. When the principle on which a society operates is that a person's skin color determines the amount of respect he warrants, then it's consistent with that principle to have rules of etiquette that reinforce that view. People who accepted that principle and employed different honorifics for people of different races were thus acting in a consistent way. Of course, the principle that respect-worthiness depends on skin color is morally abhorrent, and our society's ever-so-gradual recognition of this has led to accompanying changes in our social behavior. The need for changes in our social practices is driven by the need to change the underlying principle and achieve consistency between the principle and the conventions that express it. As our views about equality evolved, so have our conventions about forms of address.

If we read King's letter, which is primarily addressed to white pastors, we see that his strategy includes pointing out to them the connections between the moral ideals of respect and equality and the specific practices of society at that time. In the letter, he suggests that if they are as committed to the principle of racial equality as they profess themselves to be, then they need to change the way in which they are acting (or failing to act) on it. Part of the effectiveness of the letter depends on the fact that he appeals to their shared moral and religious views in pleading for their support for his efforts. He argues that reflection on the principles that they already hold, or at least claim to hold, will prove him to be justified in demanding immediate reforms in both the law and in social practices.

In this way, the principles of manners give us a powerful way of critiquing specific social conventions and rules of etiquette. We can now see that withholding honorifics on the basis of skin color is deeply disrespectful. Thus, the people who refused to act on that convention in the past were justified in disregarding the existing rules. Were they acting rudely? Not necessarily. Martin points out that using etiquette "to correct, embarrass, or demean others is the height of rudeness."[11] The rules of etiquette are supposed to serve the aims of morality, not the other way around.

If, as I have argued, the rules of etiquette get their justification from underlying moral principles, then it follows that an etiquette rule that is at odds with a moral principle is not in fact a binding rule, no matter how many etiquette books include it. So a person who addressed a black married woman as "Mrs." in the 1950s may have been violating an existing convention, but she would not have been acting rudely.

This is probably not the sense in which most people use the word "rude." For most people, rude behavior is whatever violates the actual rules of etiquette in use in their society. In this book, however, I will take for granted that rude behavior is behavior that reflects bad moral principles or an inconsistency with good moral principles that we think a person should be able to recognize. A person who really does think that blacks and whites are equal, but who continues to use the old forms of address, is behaving rudely. This is not just because she is following an outdated convention that nearly everyone else has dropped, but because we now think it ought to be obvious to everyone that this is disrespectful behavior.

A similar point can be made about the employment of etiquette as a kind of litmus test for whether someone is the "right sort" for a job, a dinner party, or a marriage. Certainly the ability to distinguish a pickle fork from an oyster fork depends on having being exposed to a style of living in which people eat oysters in the first place and do not just pick up pickles with their fingers. If etiquette rules are primarily ways of sustaining and enforcing morally objectionable boundaries between social classes, it is hard to defend them. After all, our sympathies are properly with the Eliza Doolittles of the world, not Henry Higgins.

But on the view I am defending, the politeness of an action depends on the extent to which it reflects correct underlying moral principles and attitudes. This means that some widely followed conventions of etiquette may prove to be deeply misguided and hence, ought to be rejected. It also means that when someone uses an otherwise acceptable rule of etiquette for immoral purposes, such as deliberately setting a table with an unusual array of forks so as to trip someone up, they are acting rudely. It's true that people do sometimes try to employ etiquette in order to embarrass or humiliate others by putting their ignorance on display. What I deny is that they are acting politely in doing so. As Martin puts it,

> To sacrifice the principles of manners, which require compassion and respect, and bat people over the head with their ignorance of etiquette rules they cannot be expected to know is both bad manners and poor etiquette. That social climbers and twits have misused etiquette throughout history should not be used as an argument for doing away with it. Worse villains have misused the law to promote injustice, but the majesty of the law manages to survive. You don't judge a system by the people who abuse it.[12]

The person who deliberately employs social conventions to convey morally dubious attitudes is acting rudely. The politeness of a given action is tied to the underlying moral aim, not to the behavior itself. Following existing rules of etiquette is rude when the aim is to express disrespect or humiliate someone. Likewise, flouting existing rules is not rude when flouting them is the best way to express respect and consideration. This explains why Queen Victoria would have been acting politely, not rudely, in drinking from her finger bowl when her dinner guest, unfamiliar with finger bowls, mistook his for a glass.[13]

Etiquette experts generally agree that taking public note of another's etiquette lapse is itself a lapse of etiquette. Even if you do use the oyster fork to get yourself a pickle, no one else is supposed to notice, much less call anyone's attention to your mistake. This is not always possible; as we know from experience, pretending not to see something can occasionally make things worse. (Presumably Queen Victoria thought that ignoring the finger bowl issue would not be sufficient to spare her guest embarrassment, which is why she took more drastic measures.) I will have more to say about this in Chapter 4.

The implication of the view I have been defending is that as our moral attitudes evolve and change, so should our social conventions. The change in etiquette rules about addressing blacks and whites was brought about by a change in our society's way of understanding what it means to treat people equally. But such changes do not happen all at once, and when moral attitudes are in the process of evolving, the result can be considerable confusion and conflict about which social conventions should be followed and what the following of those conventions communicates.

In American culture, this is perhaps most noticeable when it comes to social conventions about interactions between men and women, particularly in public places. If letters to etiquette columnists are any indication, we are experiencing considerable angst about practices like opening doors and relinquishing seats on public transportation. The question of whether a man should hold a door open for a woman causes considerable disagreement, in part because it's just not clear what message is being conveyed by that act. Does it show respect, or does it imply disrespect by suggesting that a woman isn't capable of opening doors on her own?

People opposed to door-opening for women argue that this convention, like the convention about addressing black men and women by their first names, rests on an assumption of moral inequality between men and women. (Let's assume that we are not talking about an unreasonably cumbersome door.) This has always struck some people as a strange argument— how could holding a door open for someone express an attitude of superiority? Isn't it quite the opposite? A tribute to women? Certainly many men view it this way. Critics respond by saying that putting women on a pedestal is not the same as respecting them. They might point to the rather similar arguments used to deny women voting rights, arguments which claimed that giving the vote to women would destroy their moral purity. This is not really treating women as equals, even though it sounds a lot better than arguing that women aren't rational enough to vote, as others claimed.

What a given man intends to convey through opening a door for a woman no doubt depends on many factors. Plenty of men were simply brought up that way and have trouble relinquishing such ingrained habits. They may also fear that not opening a door would show disrespect. Indeed, the decision about whether to open a door for a woman whose views on door opening aren't known has become a bit of a catch-22. He may worry about offending her no matter what he does.

This convention gets worked out differently in different contexts. Some men open doors for women they know, but not for strangers. Others open doors for older women, but not for younger women. Still others—men and women—have adopted the practice of opening doors for everybody, regardless of gender. Of course, we can't have it as our rule that each of us always lets the other go through a door first, since that would mean that no one ever actually walks through a door. In situations that do not permit much time for deliberation or discussion, it is practical to have some rule or other. Having widely recognized rules about the order in which people get on and off elevators or subway trains is obviously useful. Most people now seem to employ rules that the person nearest the door gets off first, and that people provide extra assistance to anyone who might appear to need it, whether it is an elderly man, a pregnant woman, or a father pushing a double stroller. It is not a perfect system, but at least it doesn't require five men to plaster themselves against the walls of an elevator just so that a woman in the back can proceed ahead of them.[14] When a social convention is in flux, politeness probably requires being patient and not ascribing malevolent intentions to people who do not appear to be harboring any. Individual acts of door opening and seat offering should normally be met with polite gratitude rather than rudeness, even if the offers are declined as unnecessary. This is because in most cases, the person following the convention means well, and good manners requires that we acknowledge this.

The intention with which an action is undertaken makes a difference to whether it is respectful or not. This is not to say that it's permissible to violate rules of etiquette if your intentions are good—just that intentions have an effect on what is communicated. As we all know, the tone of voice in which something is said can radically change what is conveyed. If my use of the word "please" when I ask you to pass the salt is dripping with sarcasm, I am obviously not communicating my respect for you as a Kantian end. The success of the communication depends not simply on the convention, but also what the communicator intends to convey and what message the object of the communication receives.

Let's return to honorifics. King's letter reflects the view at the time that "Mrs." was the most respectful way of addressing a married woman. Many people continue to take this view today. But many others, particularly younger women, do not. Not all women change their names when they marry, and even women who do change their names often dislike being addressed as "Mrs. Alistair Hullabaloo." They may prefer "Mrs. Millicent Hullabaloo" or "Ms. Millicent Hullabaloo" or "Senator Millicent Hullabaloo." How do we resolve this? Do we address Grandma as "Ms. Esmeralda Persnickety" when she calls herself "Mrs. Edgar Persnickety?" Can Grandma address mail to her physician grandson and his wife as "Dr. and Mrs. Martin Modern" if she is governor of a state? When a convention is so much in flux, how are we supposed to know what is really polite?

The advice of Miss Manners on this point is that everyone should abide by a person's known preferences, on the grounds that ignoring them conveys a lack of concern for the addressee's attitudes. Abiding by a person's known preference is itself a way of communicating respect for that person. Likewise, ignoring known preferences is clearly disrespectful, and therefore rude. So Grandma is "Mrs. Edgar Persnickety" and her grandson and his wife are "The Honorable Marvela Withthetimes" and "Dr. Martin Modern." If preferences aren't known, we are to make reasonable guesses as to what those preferences would be, and act accordingly. On the flip side, no one should take offense at another person's reasonable guess.

Blatant disregard for the rules of etiquette is rude, but genuine confusion is not, or at least not always. Undoubtedly we are morally responsible for learning new conventions as they arise and not sticking stubbornly to the ones to which we are accustomed. A similar principle applies when visiting countries where quite different etiquette rules may be in operation. The presumption according to just about all etiquette experts is that the customs of the culture in which one is in should prevail when possible. Newcomers are granted leeway as they learn the conventions, but they are responsible for learning them as quickly as possible and acting on them so far as they can.[15]

This much may seem like common sense, but of course, matters are not always so simple. Some of a country's more important conventions may not be written down anywhere, and indeed, might not even be recognized as rules by those who follow them. For example, different cultures have very different conventions about how close one may stand to someone else without violating that person's space and making him or her uncomfortable. Americans tend to keep more distance than people in other cultures, and so a person from a country where the custom is to stand close by may inadvertently offend an American. Likewise, the American's probably unconscious tendency to keep her distance may be perceived as unfriendly or rude. For the most part, the only way to pick up on these conventions is through careful observation of the practices of a culture.

Cultures are not, of course, homogeneous. It's possible to make some generalizations about American social conventions, but the United States itself has many different subcultures. What counts as reasonably polite behavior in New York City may well seem appallingly rude in Savannah. The native of Georgia might feel as though he has landed in a foreign country when he steps out of Penn Station and onto a typically crowded New York sidewalk. Moreover, he may not feel willing or able to adapt his behavior to those standards, although if he doesn't adapt at least a little bit, he might be in danger of getting trampled or causing a major traffic problem. Likewise, a New Yorker whose only goal in a grocery store is to get in and out as quickly as possible is likely to run into difficulties in the checkout line in a small Southern town, where different conventions of hospitable customer service are likely to be in operation.[16]

In general, we tend to think that people should simply adapt to the environment in which they find themselves. The visitor to New York City should step up his pace on the sidewalk, even if it's not the way he would prefer to walk. And the New Yorker should work on controlling his impatience when shopping in a Southern grocery store. As the saying goes, "when in Rome, do as the Romans do."

This works well enough when the differences are about the rules of etiquette, not the moral principles behind them. It is easy enough to say that when I am in Japan, I should remove my shoes on entering a house and treat business cards that I am offered respectfully rather than shoving them in a coat pocket. Here both parties believe that respect is important; the only question is the convention through which that respect is best conveyed. (The Japanese host should also be mindful of the ways that Americans typically communicate respect and accept the hearty handshake for what it is intended to be.) But not all differences in the rules of etiquette can be resolved so easily. Where the differences reflect an underlying moral disagreement, it becomes much harder to sort out which conventions should prevail.

Consider the very emotionally fraught debates in France about whether Muslim women and girls should be permitted to wear head scarves, burqas or abayas in public. Many people believe that the dress codes practiced by many Muslim women represent a morally unjustifiable view about women and their role as objects of sexual desire. Defenders of the practice reject this claim, often pointing to modesty in clothing as a practice that benefits women by ensuring them greater respect from men. The question of whether people, especially women, should adopt the clothing practices of their current location is far more complicated than the question of removing one's shoes in Japan. This is because what's in dispute is not the convention itself, but the underlying moral principle that supports it. If Jane thinks that burqas are a tool for the subjugation of women, then she may think it would be wrong of her to wear one in circumstances where wearing it might seem to express acceptance of a belief that she in fact rejects. Likewise, her hosts may be unwilling to accept her Western dress because they interpret it as disrespectful of their traditions. This is a moral dispute over what respecting women really means; it's not simply a case of conflicting etiquette rules. If I am right that the principles of manners are moral principles, then at least some debates over etiquette conventions are really disguised debates about morality. We should thus not be surprised that they generate such strong emotions and seem so difficult to settle.

In this chapter, I have argued that while the rules of etiquette are clearly conventional, that does not mean that they aren't binding on us. Their authority derives from their role in communicating important underlying moral aims like respect and consideration. Elaine and Jerry might have answered George by pointing out that when a host has gone to the trouble of planning an elaborate, sophisticated dinner party, a guest should show appreciation for this effort. Probably Elaine objects to Pepsi and Ring Dings because they are too easily obtained and, as convenience foods, would be in bad taste (a subject to which we will return in Chapter 8). She worries that bringing them would communicate the wrong message to their host, perhaps that they are not sufficiently grateful for their efforts. Of course, the show ends up poking fun at Elaine's certainty that chocolate babka is the only suitable hostess gift. Elaine's rigidity is just as much of a problem as George's skepticism. Neither of them has a very good grasp on what good manners requires of them.

Indeed, none of the characters on Seinfeld really knows very much about etiquette. They often express a great deal of certainty about the correctness of a particular convention, but they are usually challenged in that certainty by another character or by unexpected plot twists. It's not simply that they are unclear about the rules; they also have little idea about how those rules interact with underlying moral aims and goals, like expressing appreciation to a host. In short, they lack any sort of expertise about either manners or morality. In the next chapter, we will turn to the question of what such expertise consists in.

Three

I may not dispute Mrs. Post. If she says that is the way you should talk, then indubitably that is the way you should talk.[1]

Dorothy Parker

In the first chapter, I put forward the claim that the practice of good manners goes hand in hand with good moral character. In the second chapter, I argued that social conventions serve as communication devices through which we express moral attitudes and aims, like showing respect for others and consideration for their needs. Although it's true that the rules of etiquette are primarily conventional and highly susceptible to variation and change across time and culture, it doesn't follow that they are pointless or arbitrary. On the contrary, a shared understanding about the rules of etiquette is essential if we are to succeed in conveying respect and consideration through abiding by them.

But do we in fact have a shared understanding of those rules? In an episode of *Curb Your Enthusiasm*, Larry tries to pin down the cut-off time for evening phone calls.[2] Larry is convinced that it is 10:30; his wife, Cheryl, argues that it is 10:00 for people with kids. Cheryl's opinion is confirmed when Larry places a phone call at 10:20 and makes someone angry. Later, when Larry attempts to abide by the 10:00 rule, he finds himself angering someone else who thinks the cut-off time for people with kids is 9:30. All the parties involved agree that there is some point after which it is rude to call someone on the telephone. What they don't agree about is the time at which that point occurs. So although the principle of manners is not in question here, the specific rule of etiquette is. How are such disputes to be resolved?

The obvious place to turn for answers to questions like this is to etiquette experts. In the United States, Emily Post (and her descendants), Amy Vanderbilt, Letitia Baldridge, and Judith Martin are widely regarded as etiquette authorities, with their advice appearing in books, newspapers, magazines, and websites across the country. Many major news sources also employ their own experts: Philip Galanes answers etiquette questions at the New York Times, Robin Abrahams does the same at the Boston Globe, and Emily Yoffe writes on manners and morals for Slate.com. Countless other writers specialize in business manners, travel etiquette, or wedding decorum. In other words, we have no shortage of public figures and authors who, for one reason or another, have been anointed or appointed etiquette experts.

But what makes these people experts? One way to answer that question is in terms of their individual histories. What did they do or study that landed them in the position to be recognized as an expert in etiquette? Consider the background of two especially influential American etiquette writers: Emily Post and Judith Martin. Post, who was born in 1872, was a member of New York City's most elite social circles. She began her writing career as a novelist, but became known as an etiquette expert in 1922 upon the publication of the first of what would eventually be 17 editions of her best-selling book, *Etiquette in Society, in Business, in Politics, and at Home* (often called the "Blue Book" because of its distinctive blue cover). Post later became an immensely popular radio personality and wrote an etiquette column called "In Good Taste" that appeared in newspapers around the country. In 1950, a magazine poll of prominent newswomen pronounced Post the second most influential woman in America, after Eleanor Roosevelt.[3] Like Post, Judith Martin has a background in journalism, including a stint covering White House social events. Her etiquette column has been in syndication for over 30 years and her books, like Post's, have sold millions of copies. Martin's pseudonym, Miss Manners, is a household name. And yet, simply knowing the backgrounds of Post and Martin is not enough to tell us what makes their opinions about etiquette authoritative, if they are. What we really need is an account of what their expertise consists in. To put it differently, we need to consider just what it is that they know.

The question of what it means to have knowledge about something is a very old one within Western philosophy, dating back to ancient Greece. Indeed, it was the primary concern of the philosopher Socrates, at least as he is represented in the writings of his student, Plato. Socrates, who was eventually put to death by the Athenian government, took the question of expertise quite seriously. He sought out people who took themselves to be experts about matters like courage or piety, and set about questioning them to find out the extent of their knowledge about the subject. Now Socrates believed that the first step toward acquiring knowledge about a subject is ridding yourself of false beliefs about it. On his view, the better part of wisdom consists in simply acknowledging your own ignorance. His interrogations of local experts involved successive questions designed to prove to them that they did not know what they thought they did. Inevitably, the person being questioned would become confused, contradict himself, and find himself unable to say anything sensible about the topic. Socrates took himself to be doing these people a favor, since by pointing out their ignorance about a subject, he was in fact making them wiser about it. Not surprisingly, they didn't see it this way, which is why Socrates met the fate that he did.

Unlike Socrates, I am going to take for granted that at least some of the people to whom we turn for etiquette advice really do have expertise of some sort and that their expertise is based in knowledge that non-experts lack. Certainly etiquette experts know the details about specific customs, practices, and rules operating in a given culture. If I need to find out how to introduce an ambassador to my elderly grandmother or determine what's appropriate to wear for dinner at the White House, consulting a good etiquette book will likely provide me with the answer.

And yet, the expertise shown by people like Martin and Post is not something that can be entirely captured in a book, no matter how comprehensive. This is because etiquette expertise, like moral expertise, is practical. By that I mean that it has implications for the way we live. Had I written a book on, say, the daily habits of medieval Irish monks, I would certainly be an expert in that topic. But knowing everything there is to know about medieval monasteries is not likely to affect how I behave in other areas of my life. It is largely what philosophers call a form of *descriptive* knowledge, or what most non-philosophers call factual knowledge. Etiquette knowledge, like moral knowledge, is not just descriptive. It is also *normative* in that it generates conclusions about what we should do.

To say that etiquette knowledge is normative is not, however, to say that it is just a matter of opinion. After all, when Miss Manners says that something is rude, we do not simply see that as expressing her opinion in just the way that the rest of us might. Her judgments about the rudeness of an action seem to be authoritative in a way that other people's judgments generally are not. Thus, in asking what it is that etiquette experts know, we are also inquiring as to whether and how the judgments they make on the basis of that knowledge are binding on the rest of us.

So we have two questions: (1) what is the content of the etiquette expert's knowledge, and (2) how, if at all, does that knowledge generate obligations to behave in one way rather than another? To make it more concrete, we can put it this way: just how does Judith Martin know what time of night it becomes rude to place a phone call and does the fact that she has identified calling after that point as rude mean that the rest of us have reason not to do it?

Certainly, part of the content of an etiquette expert's knowledge is information about the actual traditions and practices in society. If etiquette has the communicative function for which I argued in Chapter 2, then it will have to rely on standardized conventions and rules. It's reasonable to suppose that a genuine etiquette expert will know what those standards are. Emily Post had a great deal of specific information about the rules governing the behavior of what she called "best society" or "people of quality." (When we get to the second question about authoritativeness, we will take up the question of why anyone should care about what "people of quality" do.) She was a keen observer of social customs and practices. In some senses, she was like an etiquette anthropologist—collecting and recording observed data about social behavior among a certain set of human beings and transmitting that information to others. Likewise, Judith Martin has an extensive knowledge of past customs, and she sometimes explains current rules and practices by giving an account of their history. The effect is that she is simply gathering information about longstanding, shared traditions and passing it along to readers.

And yet, it is also evident that good etiquette writers are not exclusively anthropologists or historians. Consider that Emily Post was not just an onlooker in these social gatherings she described; she was also a participant in them. One way to see her books and radio presentations is as accounts of what she and people like her do, with the implication that this is the best way to do things. This is not necessarily arrogance on Post's part; she was responding to genuine interest on the part of readers, who really did seem to want to know how she managed dinner parties, social correspondence, and the like. (Her successor in this regard is probably Martha Stewart, whose projects are presented as "what

Martha does." The stunning success of Stewart's enterprise suggests that many people are deeply interested in finding out what Martha does. I will return to Stewart in Chapter 8.) Even so, it's clear that Post was not simply giving a report of how dinner parties were managed in her social circle. She was presenting and defending an account of how people *should* behave at dinner parties, whether or not they actually do.

In the 10 editions of *Etiquette* that were published during Post's lifetime, good and bad behavior are illustrated through fictional (or semi-fictional) characters. The names of the characters indicate the extent to which their behavior is to be mimicked. For instance, Mrs. Toplofty and the Oldnames have impeccable taste, although Post clearly has a soft spot for Mr. and Mrs. Kindhart, who take pains to comfort inexperienced hostesses throwing disastrous dinner parties. Likewise, we are to avoid behaving like Mr. Parvenu and the Richan Vulgars, who have money but no real taste in either material goods or behavior. (Post's reliance on these characters changes over time. Later editions of her book feature characters like Mrs. Three-in-One, who, unlike Post but like most of her readers, lacked a household staff and hence, had to play the roles of cook, waitress, and hostess at her dinner parties.) Post employed these characters to describe the kinds of behaviors that she thought both met and fell short of the standards she was defending.

That these characters represent ideals is evident in the introduction to the 1942 edition of *Etiquette*. It contains a preface in which Post prints and answers a letter from a woman calling into question the legitimacy of using "best society" as a model. The letter-writer notes the well-publicized bad behavior of many of New York's elites, describing their behavior as "pretentious and vapid and vulgar."[4] She asks Post to say whether these are the same people that Post holds up as "best society" and, although she does not make this explicit, to defend the idea that anyone should model their conduct after them:

I do wish you would give us who are your readers a reassuring glossary for such terms as "Best Society," "Best People," "People of Quality," "People of Taste," "The Smart or the Modern, or the Fashionable World." Or if you can't, won't you be frank with us who believe you, and who are bringing our children up according to your precepts, and tell us the truth?[5]

Post, to her credit, does give the letter-writer a frank reply. She acknowledges the bad behavior and notes that people of real taste do not normally do things for which they would end up on the front page of the newspaper.[6] But the rest of Post's answer makes clear that she is not simply reporting on what people actually do, in the way that an anthropologist would. Rather, she is choosing examples and exemplars that meet her own ideals of manners:

No, I do not "make up" the people of whom I write nor the society that I define as best. But I admit that the reassuring glossary you ask for is almost as difficult to make clear as it would be to separate each color that has gone into the painting of a picture. . . . The only way for one who must for one reason or another consider the question of whether this or that group is representative is to make one's own appraisal, and from those whom one considers admirable, to make one's individual selections, and then to define that selection as Society that most nearly meets one's own idea. . . . For example, when I say that "people of taste do this, or think that," I naturally have in mind definite people whose taste is, in my own opinion, the most nearly perfect among all those whom I know. Or on occasion, perhaps, I go back in memory to the precepts of those whose excellence has remained an ideal. Or perhaps I apply recognized standards of measure—like those of the ancient

Greeks. In other words, when I write of people of quality or fashion or taste, I always select the individual people who ideally serve as models, exactly as I select flowers in my garden which are to be put in a certain bowl or vase in a certain room.[7])

What Post makes evident in this response is that her choice of exemplars is based on her own ideas about what good behavior should be. Post is thus arguing for a system of behavior, and defending it in part with largely (but not entirely) fictional examples of tasteful people. It is, in the end, her own judgment that supports her use of those examples and her claims about polite and tasteful behavior.

Post's readers certainly trusted her judgment, and that trust stemmed in part from Post's position at the top of the American social ladder. Many of Post's followers were recent immigrants, anxious to know how to fit in with their adopted culture. (Post's most serious competition was a nineteenth-century etiquette book revised and revamped by an extraordinarily talented young Jewish woman named Lillian Eichler. Eichler, who was just 19 years old when she published her first version of *The Book of Etiquette*, recognized that her appeal as an etiquette expert derived from her lack of social standing and her ability to empathize with those who felt ignorant about the rules and self-conscious about their social mistakes.[8])

Post was occasionally derided by critics as reinforcing snobbish class distinctions with her discussions of what "good society" does. But it is evident that Post took herself to be presenting an account of good taste and good manners as based in something other than simply her own judgment as a member of the upper echelons of society. This becomes increasingly apparent with each revision of her famous book, although the theme is present from the earliest edition. Good taste, on her view, is impossible without moral qualities like consideration, kindness, and attentiveness to the needs and situations of others, qualities that anyone can cultivate, regardless of social position.

Post's fictional characters are intended to carry their own authority; we are supposed to be able to see for ourselves what Mr. Richan Vulgar is doing wrong, and why the fact that Mrs. Three-in-One is serving dinner herself does not detract from her hospitality if she contrives to do it cleverly (by, for instance, keeping an ice cream maker under her chair during dinner). Likewise, it is not the old name of the Oldnames that makes their behavior and their taste flawless in Post's eyes; rather, it is the wisdom with which they deploy their resources.

In arguing for the value of etiquette, Post appeals, like Martin does, to pre-existing principles that she thinks readers will share. In Post's case, the appeal is to utility, broadly understood:

> The real point to be made is that the rules of etiquette have not been contrived in order to make those who know them seem important and to make those who happen not to know them seem miserably chagrined. Actually the so-called rules are nothing but the findings of long experience handed down for reasons of practical use. This does not mean that the principles of good taste, or of beauty, or of consideration for the rights or feelings of others can be discarded—ever! As a matter of fact, good taste is necessarily helpful! It must be the suitable thing, the comfortable thing, the useful thing for the occasion, the place, and the time, or it is not in good taste.[9]

On Post's view, conventions of etiquette and taste derive their authority from their practical value. If they are useful or make life more beautiful, they should be upheld; if they are not, they should be discarded. This is what the Oldnames understand that the Richan Vulgars do not. The Oldnames have a smaller house, but possessions that are both beautiful and perfectly suited for their purposes. Their dinner parties are less splashy, but more enjoyable and hospitable. And this is all, on Post's view, because they understand the values and principles that underlie all forms of social interaction.

Post's view about the justification of etiquette conventions is, as I said in the last chapter, supported by the account of morality defended by David Hume. For Hume, what makes a character trait a virtue is that it is either useful or agreeable to oneself or to others. Discretion, patience, and industry are virtues because of their usefulness to their possessor; honesty, benevolence, courage, and fidelity are useful to others as well. Cheerfulness, tranquility, pride, and aesthetic sensibility are immediately agreeable to the one who has them, and perhaps to others. Hume also praises those qualities that make us agreeable to others, including wit, eloquence, cleanliness, and a general sense of decorum. The rules of manners, Hume argues, make it possible for ordinary, self-centered human beings to create a functioning social world:

> the eternal contrarieties, in company, of men's pride and self-conceit, have introduced the rules of Good Manners or Politeness; in order to facilitate the intercourse of minds, and an undisturbed commerce and conversation. Among well-bred people, a mutual deference is affected: Contempt of others disguised: Authority concealed: Attention given to each in his turn: and an easy stream of conversation maintained, without vehemence, without interruption, without eagerness for victory, and without any airs of superiority. These attentions and regards are immediately *agreeable* to others, abstracted from any consideration of utility or beneficial tendencies: They conciliate affection, promote esteem, and extremely enhance the merit of the person who regulates his behavior by them.[10]

No doubt many of our social conventions are justified primarily by their utility, such as walking on the right on an American sidewalk. It is extremely helpful to be able to predict which direction a person heading toward you will move, and no doubt having such a convention both facilitates efficient sidewalk traffic flow and reduces the risk of collision between insufficiently attentive pedestrians. No such conventions apply in an uncrowded park because the collision risk is low and the need for efficiency much less.

But Hume's focus on the general agreeableness produced by an attention to good manners implies that the value of following social conventions is not simply a matter of their efficiency. Rather, Hume's claim is that we are naturally inclined to approve of people who display these characteristics, that we find them pleasant to be around. They facilitate warm human relationships and generally support the aims of morality, as Hume understood them. This idea that we are naturally disposed to find good manners agreeable will be picked up by the sociologist Erving Goffman, whose work I will discuss in the next chapter.

Let us suppose for the moment that at least some etiquette conventions do get their value from their overall social utility or agreeableness. We will not yet have fully answered the question of what makes a given etiquette rule binding on an individual, particularly when abiding by the rule would be neither useful nor agreeable to that individual. Consider, for instance, the etiquette rule that one must respond to personal invitations offering hospitality.[11] It is clearly both useful and agreeable to the host to know how many people to expect at her party, and disagreeable to have people ignore her efforts on their behalf. But perhaps the invitee finds it disagreeable to have to answer an invitation, or thinks that the host doesn't really need to know whether he is coming. Does that mean that he isn't bound by the etiquette rule?

Hume has an answer to this sort of problem, which is basically that when evaluating customs, practices, and character traits, we should take up what he calls the "general point of view." Hume recognized that we are all prone to various prejudices and biases in our personal sentiments, and that I can't base my ideas about what traits are virtues just on my own reaction to them. Rather, I need to take up a more impartial perspective and make my evaluations on what's agreeable from that perspective. Applying this to the RSVP case, the idea would be that even if I personally find it unpleasant to answer invitations, when I set that aside I can see that the practice of responding to invitations is useful and agreeable from the general point of view. And even if I am not moved by the general point of view, I can probably at least agree that people who do not answer invitations are considered disagreeable. Given the social value for me of being perceived as agreeable, that should be enough reason for me to do it.

Post, far from simply describing the practices of the people in her particular social set, aimed at spelling out the underlying justification for those practices, a justification that can be based in Hume's theory. She was quick to recognize when a given convention had lost its value to society or was becoming outmoded, such as the convention that unmarried young women required chaperones. The 1922 edition of her book takes the need for chaperones for granted, but over subsequent editions, the chaperone fades out of view. In the 1942 edition of *Etiquette*, Post points out that the practice of chaperoning young women rests on the assumption that they are in need of protection, an idea that she says is "out of tune with the world of today." Post clearly endorses this change, saying that,

> from an ethical standpoint, the only chaperon worth having in this present day is a young girl's own efficiency in chaperoning herself . . . the girl who in addition to trained judgment has the right attributes of proper pride and character needs no chaperon—ever!"[12]

Of course, in declaring chaperones no longer necessary, Post was not simply reporting on a change in social norms. She was bringing about a change in social norms. Given her stature, a declaration by Emily Post that propriety no longer demanded chaperones for young girls would have been, for many people, sufficient to make it so.

Social conventions, for Post, are not static; they must adapt to meet the changing needs of society. They must also, in her view, be put in the proper perspective. Post was no defender of fanatical adherence to the rules of etiquette. She probably would have shared Kant's disdain for "fantastically virtuous" people who allow "nothing to be morally indifferent."[13] The person who "strews her steps" with duties of etiquette is as unpleasant to be around as the person who turns everything into a moral issue, no matter how trivial. (Indeed, Post was well-known for keeping her elbows on the table as she ate, on the grounds that this particular rule simply didn't matter very much.) Rules of etiquette serve the aims of pleasant social life, not the other way around.

Post's claim to expertise, then, rests on her ability to identify social conventions that are in fact useful by making social life more pleasant and harmonious. In Chapter 8, we will see how Post, who was herself quite well versed in the principles of art and architecture, employed aesthetic standards in her judgments about good taste in decorating a house. The wisdom that many people found in Post's advice is wisdom about which conventions are important, how, when, and where they should be followed, and what point they are serving at any given time.

The idea that moral expertise is a kind of wisdom about what is valuable for human beings living in community with each other is not a new one. Indeed, it is central to Aristotle's famous account of virtue, as it is spelled out in the *Nicomachean Ethics*.[14] Aristotle's conception of virtue is quite complicated, more so than it might appear to a casual reader. Virtue, for Aristotle, is a complex amalgamation of habituated responses and finely tuned judgments, the combination of which enables agents to both identify what virtue requires and also act on the basis of that judgment. Virtuous people have genuine knowledge about what really matters in human life, and are able to apply that knowledge to particular situations that they face. This, for Aristotle, is the reason why we rightly take them to be experts.

In the remaining pages of this chapter, I will make the case that etiquette expertise is a form of moral expertise, as Aristotle understood it. What makes someone like Post or Martin a genuine etiquette expert is not simply the fact that she is knowledgeable about customs and traditions, but also that she is unusually good at identifying and articulating what the principles of manners imply about how we should behave in the complicated, messy circumstances of real life.

Early in the *Nicomachean Ethics*, Aristotle divides virtue into two types: moral and intellectual. Moral virtues, such as generosity and courage, are primarily patterns of actions and feeling. Ideally, the patterns are acquired in childhood through a process of habituation that employs the natural incentive of pleasure and the natural disincentive of pain. Take generosity. The way to inculcate generosity in a child, on Aristotle's view, is to reward generous behavior and punish selfish behavior in such a way that the child associates generous actions with pleasant experiences and selfish actions with unpleasant experiences.[15] With enough repetition, Aristotle argues, she will get into the habit of doing generous actions and what's more, she will find those actions enjoyable. Generosity will become part of her character, and because she enjoys being generous, her generous actions will provide her with pleasure.

But Aristotle recognizes that this account is insufficient as it stands. For one thing, it doesn't provide us with any way of resolving conflicts between virtues. Suppose that I am on my way to my friend Bill's house to pay him the 20 dollars that I owe him. Along the way, I encounter an elderly woman who is homeless and in need of a hot meal. If I am generous, I will undoubtedly be inclined to give her some money. On the other hand, if I am just, I will want to repay Bill. This looks like a situation where the demands of justice and the demands of generosity conflict with each other.

Even in situations where we have no conflicts between virtues, having the right habits won't be enough to ensure that we always act virtuously. A virtue like generosity, after all, is complicated in practice. We may know that we should donate money to charity, but we may be unsure which charity is most deserving, or how much money to give. Giving too little money would be stingy, but giving too much would be wasteful. Courage presents the same problem. Sometimes it's cowardly to run away from danger, but sometimes it's just plain idiotic to stand one's ground. How do we know what courage really requires of us?

For that, we need something else, and that something else in Aristotle's account is the intellectual virtue of practical wisdom. Practical wisdom is absolutely essential to Aristotle's account of virtue, but Aristotle's own account of it leaves it rather mysterious. Broadly speaking, practical wisdom is knowledge about what is good and bad for human beings. But Aristotle does not mean what is good and bad for us in narrow terms, like what does and does not contribute to high cholesterol. Rather, he means that the practically wise person understands what it takes for human beings to flourish or live well, given our strengths, limitations, and circumstances.

The practically wise person has wisdom about what is and is not worth pursuing in human life. She knows that it's worth risking one's life entering a burning building to save a child, but not to save a signed copy of Paris Hilton's autobiography. She knows what to get angry about (racist hiring policies) and what to let slide (a bad call by a referee in her second grader's soccer game). But practical wisdom is not just wisdom about what is valuable in general; it also requires the ability to see what matters in particular, concrete circumstances. Many of us know full well that we should not get angry over small things, but in practice, have a hard time distinguishing between insults and minor slights. Part of practical wisdom is the ability to recognize what matters when it is put right in front of us.

There is a third component of practical wisdom, besides general wisdom about valuable ends and the ability to see their application in practice. That third component is akin to something Aristotle called cleverness, which is a kind of means–end reasoning. The practically wise person is not simply able to recognize what is important in the situations she confronts; she is also skilled at acting in such a way that preserves and promotes what she correctly judges to be important. So it's not enough to care about family harmony and know that it's important to keep things pleasant at Thanksgiving dinner. One must also have specific skills that enable one to keep the peace, such as coming up with a suitable seating arrangement, turning the conversation away from topics that will cause arguments, and knowing when to take the brandy bottle away from Uncle Hank.

Importantly, Aristotle thought that practical wisdom is not the kind of thing that can be taught; it can only be learned through experience over time. A parent may tell her teenager many wise things about romantic relationships, but much of that wisdom will inevitably fail to sink in precisely because it is the kind of thing one has to learn for oneself. Not that everyone learns it— Aristotle thinks that experience is necessary, but not sufficient for acquiring practical wisdom. After all, there are plenty of senior citizens still making lousy relationship choices. In order to acquire practical wisdom, one needs to be willing to reflect on those experiences. And one also needs the moral virtues.

Aristotle took the view, quite controversial among contemporary philosophers, that it is impossible to have any of the moral virtues without practical wisdom, and also that it is impossible to have practical wisdom without moral virtue. I have already indicated why we need practical wisdom in order to exercise the moral virtues. It is not enough to have generous or courageous impulses; they need to be oriented in the right direction if the action is really going to be courageous or generous. The reason why we need moral virtue in order to have practical wisdom is less obvious, but Aristotle gives us a clue when he says that "virtue makes the goal correct."[16] Aristotle holds that the wisdom about ends described above is only possible if one is already attached to the right things. The child who is taught to value material possessions over friendships will never develop practical wisdom, because his attachments will forever be disordered. If he cares too much about his Xbox and too little about the feelings of his friends, he is never going to be able to weight them properly in practical decision-making.

On Aristotle's view, practical wisdom demands considerable intellectual dexterity. The moral expert is a good reasoner, both about big ethical questions and also about concrete practical circumstances. This means that the moral expert must be capable of bringing abstract moral considerations to bear in novel situations with no clear precedent. The practically wise person can see what, for instance, justice requires in circumstances she has never before encountered, because she is capable of reasoning well between the abstract principle that justice is important and the particular features of her immediate situation. Etiquette expertise requires this kind of intellectual dexterity as well. Plenty of etiquette questions posted to people like Post and Martin cannot readily be brought under existing rules of etiquette. Genuine etiquette experts must be able to adapt the rules and customs for new circumstances, according to what will actually further the moral aims underlying them.

Consider, for instance, the need to develop new rules about the polite use of electronic devices. Obviously, one cannot consult nineteenth-century etiquette books on the subject of texting at the dinner table, at least not without considerable amendment. It may be possible to fit rules about texting under rules about other forms of conversation, but texting is not an ordinary form of conversation.[17] In order to come up with new rules of etiquette, it's necessary to refer back to the principles of manners and the moral values that they represent. What good etiquette experts display is an ability to move between principles of manners and rules of etiquette in such a way that enables them to extend existing conventions and their justifications to new scenarios and circumstances. We might describe this as a kind of improvisation, and it is something that the most insightful etiquette experts do especially well.

In a letter printed in *Miss Manners' Guide to Excruciatingly Correct Behavior*, a woman asks Martin for advice about responding to someone else's humiliating social disaster. The woman and her husband were attending an elegant party on a visit to Boston, during which they witnessed the following scene:

> a lady in a low-cut gown tripped, stumbled, lurched across the table, falling face first into a bowl of guacamole dip, and in the process "popped out" of her top. After an initial silence, practically everyone in the room burst out laughing, even though it was obvious that the lady was terribly embarrassed.[18]

The letter-writer subsequently got into an argument with her husband about whether laughing was a breach of etiquette, on the grounds that it would increase the victim's embarrassment. She thought it was, but her husband said "that it was not impolite for people to laugh at something like that so long as they meant no harm and didn't 'overdo' it."[19] She writes to Miss Manners to settle the question and receives this answer:

> What do you mean "something like that"? Miss Manners doubts that there is anything in the world like an elegantly dressed Bostonian lurching across the room and diving face first into a bowl of guacamole dip while simultaneously

disengaging her bodice from her bosom. Therefore, Miss Manners has a wee bit of trouble preparing a general rule for dealing with this eventuality.[20]

Here the problem is that the proper response to such a situation, unusual as it is, cannot possibly be fully given by reference to existing rules of etiquette. In general, one ignores social disasters, but that will not do in this situation, as Martin acknowledges:

> One might try to ignore a less spectacular accident. If, say, it were avocado dip, rather than guacamole, and the lady had merely trailed her sleeve in it, one could pretend not to have noticed. To pretend not to notice a performance such as you have described—even if it were humanly possible—would be to suggest that the lady did it all the time and her friends have gotten used to it. It is far better to comfort her later by telling stories of your own about hilariously embarrassing accidents you have survived.[21]

Suppressing laughter at such a situation probably would require more self-control than most people can manage, which is why the woman should cut her husband some slack for cracking up on the spot. But there is something more to this answer. Martin's point is not simply that ignoring the incident is likely not to be possible; rather, it would also be less kind to the victim. The general principle that we show consideration for people in embarrassing situations applies, but here that principle of consideration demands that we acknowledge the incident instead of ignoring it. Ignoring minor social disasters usually helps preserve the embarrassed party's self-respect, because it makes it possible for her to go on as if it has never happened or console herself with the belief that no one noticed. But in this case, there is no way the woman can go on as if it never happened or as if no one noticed. Her self-respect is best preserved when others engage in self-deprecation by revealing embarrassing incidents of their own. I will say more about this in the next chapter. The point here is simply that the practical etiquette expertise requires the ability to improvise upon general rules when necessary to preserve or promote the moral aims behind them.

This ability to improvise also requires recognizing when to make exceptions to existing etiquette rules. Another letter to Miss Manners illustrates the point nicely:

Dear Miss Manners:

My daughter passed away after thirty-four years of marriage. My son-in-law plans on getting married again. Will he still be my son-in-law and will his new wife be my daughter-in-law? He keeps saying he will always be my son-in-law, and she tells me she will be my daughter-in-law. Will this be? They are very good and dear to me and help me out in many ways, as I live alone and am eighty-five years old. They pick me up to visit them and bring me home again, and tell me I don't need an invitation to visit them.

Gentle Reader:

Yes, he will always be your son-in-law, and she will be your daughter-in-law. This does not necessarily apply to other people in a similar situation, and in fact rarely does. But if anyone tries to tell you that it doesn't apply to you, send them to Miss Manners, who will deal with them very severely.[22]

Technically, this is an incorrect application of the rule, but it is also obvious that this is a case where no decent person would care about the correct application of the rule. Martin writes as if she is declaring this to be an exception by fiat, but in fact she is not. Instead, she is appealing to an unstated moral principle, which is that it would be deeply unkind to disrupt the happiness of a vulnerable elderly woman or interfere with a caring relationship simply to press a point about the correct labels for relationships. In general, we should be clear about referring to relatives properly, but sometimes it just doesn't matter very much.

What Post, Martin, and other etiquette experts worth reading have is not simply knowledge of rules; rather, what they have is the capacity to see how the rules pertain to a given situation and what the effects of applying them will be. Martin's answer to the guacamole disaster letter does not explicitly take up the perspective of the unfortunate woman who landed in the guacamole, but her answer depends on her ability to appreciate how the situation will seem to her, and not just to the bystanders. The goal is to reduce the victim's embarrassment, and this is a case where her embarrassment will not be reduced, as it might be in other cases, by pretending that the incident never happened.

This kind of empathetic imagining is essential to knowing what good manners require of us in a concrete situation. It is one thing to know that etiquette instructs hosts to do whatever necessary to avoid embarrassing guests, but it is another thing to know what kinds of things they are likely to find embarrassing. In order to do that, we need to be able to put ourselves in the embarrassed guest's place so that we can grasp what she might need from us. We also need to be able to pull off the actions that would in fact reduce her embarrassment.

How do we develop this imaginative capacity? Lord Chesterfield's letters provide some insight here. One of the many striking things about the letters is the emphasis Chesterfield places on paying attention to one's surroundings. Recognizing, as he must, that he cannot possibly provide young Philip with a complete set of rules about how to behave across a wide range of social circumstances, he instead urges him to cultivate habits of observation:

> without attention nothing is to be done; want of attention, which is really want of thought, is either folly or madness.

> You should not only have attention to everything, but a quickness of attention, so as to observe, at once, all the people in the room, their motions, their looks, and their words, and yet without staring at them, and seeming to be an observer. This quick and unobserved observation is of infinite advantage in life, and is to be acquired with care.[23]

This quote might well be taken as further evidence of Chesterfield's cynicism, but there is another reading as well, one in which Chesterfield is urging Philip to engage in a kind of reflective awareness of the world around him. It is not that Chesterfield thinks that traditional moral education, acquired through traditional methods like reading with a tutor, is unimportant. Rather, he thinks it incomplete:

> Do not imagine that the knowledge which I so much recommend to you, is confined to books, pleasing, useful, and necessary as that knowledge is: but I comprehend in it the great knowledge of the world, still more necessary than that of books. In truth, they assist one another reciprocally; and no man will have either perfectly, who has not both. The knowledge of the world is only to be acquired in the world, and not in a closet. Books alone will never teach it to you; but they will suggest many things to your observation, which might otherwise escape you.[24]

I think we can make the case that Chesterfield is here advocating for something like Aristotle's practical wisdom when it comes to knowledge acquired through books and knowledge acquired through experience of the world. Books tell us where to look, but we cannot learn about human nature and human society unless we do observe.[25]

The ability to attend to our circumstances when necessary is one of the more central aspects of good manners. Indeed, many forms of rude behavior are really forms of inattentiveness: texting while walking down a busy sidewalk, letting a door slam in someone's face, failing to notice that someone in need of a seat has entered the waiting room or gotten on the subway. It is not that being attentive is the whole of manners, but it is certainly an important starting point. (It is also, as we shall see in later chapters, an essential element of that indispensable social virtue we call tact.)

Of course, good manners can also require that we feign a lack of attention, such as when someone has suffered a medical emergency in which we are not needed to assist. In such situations, politeness requires that we avoid attending to something that quite naturally draws our interest. But here the inattention is a deliberate choice, and it is a choice that can only be made by someone who sees the event that she subsequently judges she should ignore. It is thus quite different than the behavior of someone so wrapped up in his thoughts or his BlackBerry that he fails to notice the emergency at all. The person who notices the emergency and, after judging that she can be of no help, ignores it is acting politely by not staring. The person with his eyes glued to his BlackBerry is simply not acting rudely by not staring.

Etiquette expertise, thus, requires a complex set of skills. A genuine etiquette expert knows the principles of manners and understands their moral basis. She also knows the corresponding rules of polite behavior applicable in a given situation. So an etiquette expert will know how to greet someone respectfully in a variety of cultural settings. But her expertise, if she is really good at her job, extends beyond these matters. For she is also skilled at attending to the specific features of the situation and improvising on the standard rules when that becomes necessary. She is capable of taking up the perspective of other people, figuring out what are the effects of various actions, and settling on the particular course of behavior that will best promote the underlying moral aims of manners in those circumstances.

Let us grant that someone like Judith Martin deserves to be called an expert in etiquette both because of what we might describe as her book knowledge of the rules and her ability to put those rules into practice in concrete, often highly specific situations. That doesn't settle the question of what makes her claims authoritative. People who write to Miss Manners presumably do so because they want her advice. Her answers to them carry authority in part because they have likely made a decision to abide by what she says. But what about the rest of us? If I didn't ask for her advice, why should I care what Miss Manners thinks that her letter-writers should do?

In Martin's case, the answer is provided by an appeal to the principles of manners themselves, although she rarely makes this explicit. But if what she is doing is drawing conclusions about specific actions based on those principles, then assuming that she has reasoned well, her judgment that an action is rude draws its authority from the underlying principles and her ability to make clear how they apply to a given situation. The implicit expectation is that we share her commitment to those underlying principles. If we do not, then her judgment does not have authority for us. Post too presumes that we are all responsible for contributing to the beauty and smooth functioning of society. If we reject this view, then what Post has to say is not likely to move us.

My guess is that most people who do not take etiquette seriously do so primarily because they take an unreasonably narrow view of it, or because it seems like a matter of common sense. Etiquette writers who lack the intellectual dexterity of Post and Martin probably do little to bolster the case for etiquette, since their answers often seem either arbitrary or obvious. But good etiquette writers can make explicit the connections between our deepest moral commitments and our behavior in ordinary social interactions. They do not simply see themselves as the upholders of stiff and stuffy rules and traditions; rather they are adapting and extending those traditions in new ways to meet the changing demands of society. It is on this basis that it is reasonable to consider writers like Post and Martin as engaging in applying moral theory to everyday life, and doing so in a practically wise way.

Now it is true that etiquette experts, even very good ones, settle some questions by fiat, rather than by giving an argument for it or citing existing traditions. (Martin makes the occasional pronouncement that something is a rule because she says that it is, but she also usually acknowledges via humor the arbitrariness of her doing so.) Sometimes there is no real alternative. No argument is going to take us from the principle that we should respect others' need for rest to the rule that it is always rude to place a non-emergency phone call after a certain time of night. What we need is simply a clearly stated general rule, which can be amended on a case-by-case basis by mutual agreement of the parties.[26] Etiquette experts are in a position to create such rules and make them widely known. Of course this works best when we have only one dominant etiquette expert or else a set of experts who agree on the same rules. Otherwise, you could argue that you are following Amy Vanderbilt while I am waving a Miss Manners column. Regardless, the ability to cite the authority of a known etiquette expert is usually enough to defend oneself against the charge of being rude or inconsiderate. Had Larry been able to find a relevant rule in an etiquette book about the cut-off time for phone calls, he would have been standing on more solid ground. (Alas for Larry, Miss Manners apparently takes the view that 9:00 is the cut-off time.[27])

On the picture I have been defending, an etiquette expert's authority rests not simply on her background or even her factual knowledge of actual customs. Rather, it rests on her ability to employ practical wisdom to apply the rules of etiquette in novel circumstances, where that requires the ability to improvise on existing rules and amend or suspend them as needed. Practically wise etiquette writers are worth listening to for the same reason that practically wise moral philosophers are worth listening to—namely, that they have something to teach us about how to live well in the world we inhabit.

I began this chapter with a quote from Dorothy Parker, but it was a somewhat misleading use of it. In the review of Post's book from which that quote is taken, Parker is actually poking fun at Post's suggestions for safe conversational topics. Here is the quote in context:

> The letters and the conversations of the correct, as quoted by Mrs. Post, seem scarcely worth the striving for. The rules for the finding of topics of conversation fall damply on the spirit. "You talk of something you have been doing or thinking about—planting a garden, planning a journey, contemplating a journey, or similar safe topics. Not at all a bad plan is to ask advice: 'We want to motor through the South. Do you know about the roads?' Or, 'I'm thinking of buying a radio. Which make do you think is best?'"
>
> I may not dispute Mrs. Post. If she says that is the way you should talk, then, indubitably, that is the way you should talk. But though it be at the cost of that future social success I am counting on, there is no force great enough ever to make me say, "I'm thinking of buying a radio."[28]

It's worth noting that Parker is not taking issue with Post's standing to determine which conversational topics are safe; rather, she is criticizing the value that Post places on safe conversational topics. I think it is unlikely that Post herself would have said that we should limit our social conversations to roads and radios; presumably she is talking about finding opening gambits for conversations with strangers whose own tastes and preferences are unknown. Still, we might reasonably infer that Post and Parker disagree about what makes a person agreeable or a dinner party successful. The dispute is not about Post's authority as an etiquette expert, or even about the efficacy of those rules in keeping social gatherings tranquil and orderly. Parker's challenge is directed to the value of conducting a tranquil, orderly social life in the first place. One way to read Parker's critique is that she simply thinks that Post's version of polite society is boring and superficial. In the next chapter, we will take up the question of whether she is correct.

Self-presentation

Four

> She had the comfort of appearing very polite while feeling very cross.[1]
>
> Jane Austen

For every person who reads a Jane Austen novel and longs for the courteous social exchanges represented in those works, even between people who dislike each other intensely, there is someone else who finds such manners unbearably stiff, formal, and perhaps even hypocritical. Why should Emma find it so comforting that she is able to be polite to Mr. Elton? After all, he is the one responsible for making her feel cross in the first place by his annoying behavior at the Westons' Christmas dinner party. Maybe if she had just told him directly to stop following her around and leave her in peace, he would have thought twice about proposing to her on the way home, saving everyone considerable grief.

One of the primary contemporary objections to etiquette as a normative force in society is the idea that its rules impose on us an artificial standard of behavior, one that doesn't reflect who we really are or what we really think. Good manners, it might be argued, prevent us from being ourselves. Politeness demands that we present a public façade that covers up our real attitudes, opinions, and feelings. But why should we have to go to this trouble? What's the point of concealing our feelings and opinions from others? Isn't society more honest, open, and even more productive when we know where everyone stands and when we feel free to express ourselves and our opinions candidly?[2]

Emma is very polite to Mr. Elton. So polite, in fact, that she accidentally misleads him into thinking that she is interested in marrying him. Her well-honed skill at being tactful leads him to interpret her charming behavior as meaning something other than it does. This potential for good manners to interfere with open, sincere human relationships was remarked on by Emily Post herself:

> Tact, of course, means quick awareness of the feelings of others, and consideration for them. There is only one flaw in this otherwise most charming of human attributes, the possibility of insincerity. We don't know where we stand with one who diplomatically tells us only what he thinks we'd like to hear, instead of giving us a frank, straightforward answer.[3]

Post goes on to defend tact, but she recognizes that it comes with a significant cost. The public face that good manners asks us to put on for each other means that we cannot tell honesty from insincerity, frankness from flattery.

In her novel, *The Age of Innocence*, Edith Wharton portrays a society which values propriety above just about everything else. Adherence to its standards of proper behavior is an absolute requirement, and people who do not fit themselves into the prescribed mold are outcasts. The novel's protagonist, Newland Archer, and his wife May are at the center of this social world. They represent an ideal within that society, but their relationship is stunted and hindered by its expectations. May is the "perfect" wife, but Newland is torn between his desire to be the "perfect" husband, and his passion for the Countess Olenska, who either cannot or will not live in the world that Newland and May inhabit.

Newland and May, despite years of marriage, know very little about each other. The strict standards of decorum that keep their social world afloat prevent them from achieving anything like the intimacy that we think a good marriage ought to have. By contrast, Newland is able to strike up a deeply intimate relationship with the Countess. The strength of their relationship, however, depends on their being willing to flout all kinds of social conventions, although neither of them is fully able to relinquish their hold on them.

The social world that Wharton describes is, to put it mildly, unappealing.[4] No one wants to end up like Newland Archer, who spends a lifetime married to someone with whom he almost never has a candid conversation. On the other hand, in the age of *Real Housewives* and Twitter, the old saying, "familiarity breeds contempt" resonates as much as ever. It has never been so easy to find out so much about other people, both friends and strangers. And what we learn are often things that we would rather not know.

Most of us now live in the public eye more than we ever did before. We can Google an old flame or a new one, and we can check out a new colleague's Facebook page before we ever see her face in the office. Reality television shows and blogs make it possible for us to peer into the personal lives of complete strangers. Likewise, many of us now deliberately reveal far more about ourselves to both friends and strangers than was even possible in the past. More than 500 million of us have Facebook pages, and many of us have neglected to adjust our privacy settings, making our weekend party pictures available to the world. We can broadcast our current location via GPS and we can tweet every passing thought to an anonymous audience, so long as it can be expressed in 140 characters or less. The amount of formerly private information now publicly available is simply mindboggling.

There are good reasons to appreciate the informal openness that characterizes contemporary social life. It has reduced or eliminated destructive stigmas about a wide range of personal matters, such as sexual orientation or health issues. Setting aside these obvious benefits, we may still wonder whether the pendulum has swung too far, whether the Information Age has turned into the Too Much Information Age. People certainly do tweet or post on Facebook controversial things that in the past would have been kept private. In 2009, an American woman named Penelope Trunk tweeted that she was in the middle of having a miscarriage. The story made the news around the world. Many people criticized her as having crossed a line, although others applauded her openness. In her own defense, Trunk pointed out that there is nothing shameful about miscarrying and hence, no particular reason to hide it or keep it back.

Many people also feel much less shame than ever before about revealing their flaws and failings to the public. A 2010 article in the "Vows" section of the *New York Times* about a couple getting married generated considerable moral outrage, both in the *Times* comments section and in the blogosphere at large. The outrage stemmed from the couple's frank acknowledgment that they had left their spouses and young children to be with each other and their willingness to share the details in the *Times*. (The two couples had previously been friends and their children were classmates.) Many commenters thought that a couple in that situation should be sufficiently ashamed of themselves that they would avoid seeking or agreeing to a public revelation about their actions.

Etiquette has always had plenty to say about the appropriateness of seeking and revealing information about both ourselves and others, and for the most part, the rules are fairly conservative. It is hard to imagine Emily Post approving of the miscarriage tweet or the "Vows" article. But perhaps this just shows that etiquette hasn't caught up with the times, that its emphasis on privacy and decorum threatens to send us back to the world of Newland Archer. Social networking has changed the world in obvious ways, as have blogs, Twitter, and reality television. Maybe our way of interacting with both friends and strangers has been permanently altered by technology and we need new etiquette rules to reflect this. Or—just maybe—the extent to which our lives are now open to the perusal of others makes etiquette rules about privacy and self-presentation more important than ever.

In this chapter, I will consider the moral underpinnings of etiquette norms governing self-presentation in the twenty-first century. But I will begin in the eighteenth century with Immanuel Kant, who had some interesting thoughts about how people should present themselves to others and why. Reserve about certain aspects of ourselves is important, he thought, because it enables us to maintain both self-respect and the respect of others. Using Kant's ideas, I will argue that making an effort to put on a polite public face is not just practically useful, but a moral obligation. Parker may be right that Post's idea of pleasant society is boring, but she may be underestimating the moral value of keeping the unsavory parts of our lives out of public view.

In a somewhat offhand remark, Kant says that "if all men were good, there would be no need for reserve, but since they are not, we must keep the shutters closed."[5] Kant, whose approach to ethics reflects his own upbringing in an austere form of Lutheranism, took for granted that human beings are fundamentally flawed creatures. We are prone to moral failures, largely because of our tendency to act on our inclinations rather than by reason. This is not exactly a criticism of human nature; it is simply, for Kant, an honest portrayal of what we are like. At the same time, Kant was also a great optimist about the possibility of overcoming these failings and making genuine moral progress, both as individuals and as a society.

Kant's remarks about reserve are best understood against this background. His claim that we need to keep our shutters closed is based on his view that there are inevitably aspects of our characters and our lives that cannot bear the light of day. Judith Martin takes a similar approach when defending etiquette against the charge that it demands us to conceal or at least distract attention away from some feature of our "real" selves. Martin argues that this is an excellent thing, because the truth of the matter is that our real selves are often not fit for public display:

> Constant and universal altruism is necessarily the premise on which the most common challenge to etiquette is posed by those who have noticed that etiquette is artificial. Rather than allowing free expression, they note disdainfully, etiquette puts a sly spin, if not a dizzying turnabout, on truly harbored emotions to make people simulate emotions that are considered socially acceptable.
>
> For the moment, let us ignore the perhaps faulty research that led to this touching faith in human nature. Miss Manners needs that moment anyway, to be helped up off the floor, having been overcome with hilarity at the idea that normal people's emotions are reliably presentable. Even if it were true that no one ever felt a flicker of feeling that required a polite cover-up lest it cause mayhem, etiquette would have a mighty peacekeeping job to do. It would still have to make up for our disgracefully bad sense of timing.[6]

Martin goes on to argue that the conventions of etiquette are what enable us to behave in appropriate ways, regardless of how we are feeling at the moment when action is required. She takes for granted that our private feelings and attitudes are not always what they should be, and moreover, that it is a good thing for us to be able to hide them when necessary, say, to avoid hurting someone's feelings. (Whether this permission should extend to flat-out lying in order to spare a person's feelings is a subject we'll tackle in the next chapter.)

But there's more to the issue of reserve than hiding one's dislike of horribly ugly presents or barely edible food offered by one's host. Kant seems to be arguing for the adoption of a kind of public moral persona, one that does not accurately reflect what we are like behind the scenes. On his view, there are things about ourselves that we just shouldn't make public:

> Every house keeps its dustbin in a place of its own. We do not press our friends to come into our water-closet, although they know that we have one just like themselves. Familiarity in such things is the ruin of good taste. In the same way we make no exhibition of our defects, but try to conceal them.[7]

Kant acknowledges that everyone has faults. What he denies is that exposing our faults to the world is a good thing, either for us or for humanity in general. This may surprise readers already familiar with Kant's writings on deception. As we will see in the next chapter, the vehemence of Kant's opposition to lying is nearly unparalleled in philosophy. On what grounds could he justify hiding from the world information about what we are really like?

For Kant the answer lies in the effects that the revelation of those defects has on how we perceive ourselves and how others perceive us. A fully candid self-presentation, he thinks, is likely to cast me in a rather unflattering light:

> we have certain natural frailties which ought to be concealed for the sake of decency, lest humanity be outraged. Even to our best friend we must not reveal ourselves, in our natural state as we know it ourselves. To do so would be loathsome.[8]

> Man is reserved in order to conceal faults and shortcomings which he has; he pretends in order to make others attribute

to him merits and virtues which he has not . . . Many of our propensities and peculiarities are objectionable to others, and if they became patent we should be foolish and hateful in their eyes.[9]

Kant is not specific about what these frailties, faults, short-comings, defects, propensities, and peculiarities are, or why others would find them objectionable or indecent. Moreover, he does not give us any reason to suppose that others would be justified in finding us foolish or hateful for having them. If we are all flawed, and especially if we are all flawed in more or less the same ways, why should anyone be outraged when we acknowledge it?

Kant's point, however, is about the open display of these flaws, not the possession of them. His suggestion is that there is something morally troublesome about making our flaws public, particularly when we do so deliberately and unapologetically. In this chapter, I will argue that Kant is largely right about this, that we have moral reason to present a polite public face to the world.

The twentieth-century sociologist Erving Goffman, who produced ground-breaking work on the subject of social behavior and self-presentation, argued that our behavior in public is a kind of stage performance. When we are engaging with other people, we put on what Goffman called a front:

> I have been using the term "performance" to refer to all the activity of an individual which occurs during a period marked by his continuous presence before a particular set of observers and which has some influence on the observers. It will be convenient to label as "front" that part of the individual's performance which regularly functions in a general and fixed fashion to define the situation for those who observe the performance. Front, then, is the expressive equipment of a standard kind intentionally or unwittingly employed by the individual during his performance.[10]

Fronts are ways of presenting ourselves to others, usually with the aim of controlling how we are seen by those others. It is a form of impression management, sometimes conscious and sometimes not. Most people are familiar with deliberately adopted fronts from job interviews and similar experiences. Savvy jobseekers know the importance of behaving professionally during the interview, wearing an outfit appropriate for the environment in which you want to be hired, and putting your "best foot forward," as the expression goes.

But Goffman thinks that our employment of fronts extends well beyond limited performances like job interviews. Indeed, he argues that just about all of our social interactions are characterized by fronts. When I am in a classroom, I am presenting the front of a college professor; when I am volunteering in my daughter's classroom, I am presenting the front of an involved mother. I am, of course, still a mother when I'm teaching a college philosophy class and still a college professor when I'm helping kindergarteners construct turkeys out of pine cones. But Goffman argues that I will present myself differently in those two contexts. I will dress differently, perhaps speak differently, and generally behave in the way that I think a person occupying that role in that context ought to behave.

Fronts, on Goffman's view, involve both behavior and setting. Suppose I am having a dinner party and want to present myself as a serene, organized hostess. If I am to succeed in that front, I need to act the part by, say welcoming guests at the door in a collected fashion, remembering to take their coats, offer them drinks, and so forth. But if I appear frazzled when I answer the door, if golf clubs fall out of the coat closet when I open it, or if I have to rummage around in the basement for wine glasses, my front of being an organized hostess will have obvious cracks in it. The guests will end up with a very different impression than I am trying to put forward. So whether the front is effective depends both on what I express through my behavior and also on what is observable in the surrounding setting.

Neither my behavior nor my setting is, of course, fully under my control. I might have gotten out the wine glasses in advance, but I may not be able to control whether I have a frazzled expression on my face. Indeed, careful observers have access to all kinds of information about me beyond what I am attempting to project. In his book, *Snoop: What Your Stuff Says About You*, psychologist Sam Gosling argues that an observant visitor to someone's living quarters can leave with a great deal of information about the inhabitant's personality.[11] The kind of artwork on the walls, the position of books in the room, the presence of a to-do list and the items on it—all these things tell others a great deal about us. We of course think of our spaces as expressive of our personalities and tastes, a topic to which I will return in Chapter 8. But if they are really as revelatory as Gosling argues, then perhaps our fronts aren't all that effective. My guests may quickly figure out that I am not nearly as organized a hostess as I would like to be thought. Still, the fact that I am clearly making an effort to be one tells them something about my personality and, if I am fortunate, motivates them to help me maintain the front I am trying to put on.

This is because, as Goffman notes, the success of my front depends not just on what I do, but also on what members of my audience do. Goffman suggests that audience members can employ tact, which he describes as a protective technique, as a way of helping the performer pull off her front:

> When performers make a slip of some kind, clearly exhibiting a discrepancy between the fostered impression and a disclosed reality, the audience may tactfully "not see" the slip or readily accept the excuse that is offered for it. And at moments of crisis for the performers, the whole

audience may come into tacit collusion with them in order to help them out.[12]

A tactful guest standing near the coat closet will pretend not to see the piles of stuff that have been shoved in there in an effort to clean up the living room. And if I overcook dinner, the guests may collectively present a front of their own in which they stress their strong preference for well-done food. My performance is thus a collaborative enterprise, depending not only on my ability to put forward a front, but also on my audience's willingness to accept and sustain it.

Goffman contrasts the regions where fronts are maintained with what he calls the backstage area, or the back region. Back regions operate under a different set of norms than do front regions. Sometimes, in fact, the back region is a place where the behaviors of the front region are deliberately mocked or subverted. (For instance, Goffman describes the behavior of restaurant servers who are unfailingly polite to customers while the servers are in the dining room, but who, upon setting foot into the backstage region of the kitchen, mock those same customers mercilessly.[13]) But this need not be the case; backstage can simply be the location where performers or team members can let down their hair, so to speak, and relax. As Goffman puts it:

> Backstage conduct is one which allows minor acts which might easily be taken as symbolic of intimacy and disrespect for others present and for the region, while front region conduct is one which disallows such potentially offensive behavior.[14]

It is possible to transform a region from a front region to a back region by employing backstage conduct in a context that ordinarily calls for front region norms of behavior, such as when I invite party guests into the kitchen where I am cooking a meal.

This has the immediate effect of transforming the party into something much less formal. A similar effect is produced by the immediate use of first names upon meeting someone new, a standard American convention that creates an atmosphere of informality and comparative equality. Whether this is a good thing or not, of course, depends on the value of formality and hierarchy in those circumstances. (It's worth noting that we can't distinguish front regions from back regions merely by level of formality. A "casual" backyard barbecue with one's prospective in-laws clearly demands front region behavior!)

This distinction between front regions and back regions is very useful for thinking through real-life disagreements about the standards of appropriateness for social networking vehicles like Facebook pages. To some extent, all Facebook pages are fronts, insofar as we choose what they look like. But some people regard a Facebook page as more of a front region than others. No doubt the parent or college administrator warning the 18 year-old against posting weekend party pictures is thinking of Facebook posts in terms of front region norms. They see the teenager's Facebook page as it would be seen by interviewers or others who expect front region behavior. But many Facebook users regard their online presence as something more akin to a back region. This may be because they have in fact restricted access to their page to people whom they consider to be friends or because they think that no one else would ever be interested in tracking down that information. Or it may be that they either do not recognize the distinction between front and back regions at all, or else do not regard it as particularly important.

As it happens, Gosling argues, there isn't a lot of difference between how people present themselves on Facebook and how they present themselves in real life.[15] This is in part because although we may be under the illusion that we are fully in control of how we appear to others on Facebook, in fact we are not. We can control what we post, but not what others see. If I post a lot on Monday mornings, but never on Tuesday evenings, I may reveal myself to be a person with a procrastination problem who also happens to be a fan of the television show *Glee*. Few of us bother to track our own movements that way, just as few of us bother to arrange our books so as to make ourselves to appear more interested in, say art history, than we are. And yet, if Gosling is right, these things form part of the impression we give to others.

Disagreement about the proper boundary between front and back regions is also apparent in debates over reality television. Traditionally, of course, television shows that put themselves forward as entertainment were staffed by actors inhabiting clearly fictional roles. Reality television has turned that model of entertainment on its head. Now what we find are people who are technically playing themselves on television, but who are also often amplifying aspects of their personalities, or allowing them to be amplified by the production crew, to create a new kind of semi-fictional character. Are the Real Housewives of New Jersey actually like that in real life? Probably (hopefully!) not. And yet the fact that they purport to be real people is the appeal of the show. This is because what they reveal for us is behavior that, in ordinary life, tends to be kept backstage.

Goffman thought that fronts were an inevitable part of human social life. Impression management is a large part of what we naturally do as human beings. For better or for worse, all our interactions with other people involve fronts of some kind or other. My Facebook page is one kind of front and my behavior in Starbucks is another. But we might wonder whether there are any moral considerations governing the adoption of one front over another. More specifically, could we have moral reason to adopt a certain kind of front, one that hides our flaws, our bad habits, and our uncharitable thoughts behind a veil of politeness? In other words, could Kant be right that we have reason to keep the shutters closed on our flaws?

As Kant well knew, there is a gap between what we actually are like and what we believe we should be like and likewise, a gap between what others are like and how we ought to regard them. What putting on a polite public face (a kind of Goffman-style front) does is help us bridge that gap. The veneer of cheerfulness and good will that politeness instructs us to adopt when we are feeling grumpy or overburdened or unappreciated is not, on this view, a kind of hypocrisy. Rather it is a way of expressing our commitments to important moral ideals in the face of our own weaknesses and failings. I may not be able to summon up the gratitude that I should be feeling, or hide the envy that I am feeling, but I can at least say the right words and act as I think I should. I can engage with other people in the way that reflects my actual moral commitments. And by cooperating with other people in their efforts to put on a polite front, I enable them to live up to their own commitments. Together, we can create a front region in which we can at least put on the appearance of behaving as we really believe we should.

If it's true that certain failings must be concealed as a matter of good manners, then it must be because displaying those failings interferes with the moral aims that good manners express. In other words, there is something morally valuable about putting on a front of politeness in Goffman's sense. I suggest that the front of good manners is morally important because it expresses our status as an end in Kant's sense. This gives us moral reason to preserve our own front of polite behavior, as well as the polite fronts that other people present to us. In doing so, we treat ourselves and others with respect.

Kant, as we saw in Chapter 1, bases his claim that human beings are ends in the fact of our rational capacities. To be an end is to have dignity rather than price and absolute rather than conditional value. Presumably, then, the flaws we have reason to hide and which others may find outrageous or indecent are those flaws which present us in a way inconsistent with that status. I should conceal any habits or tendencies that would lead others to think of me as being something other than an end with dignity.

There are self-interested reasons for this. If I am totally unwilling to put on any kind of public front, I will probably miss out on many important human activities. I won't be invited to parties, offered jobs, sought out for advice, admired and honored, and so forth. But although Kant himself doesn't really attend to this, there are other kinds of reasons for doing this, reasons more closely related to self-respect and respect for others.

Kant believed that we all have a duty of self-improvement. On his view, I should constantly be striving to be a better person, both in terms of my moral character and in terms of my talents. Of course, being human, I often fail at this. But it is important that I express my ongoing commitment to those ideals and my desire to live up to them. When I make my flaws public, with no effort to hide them or offset them by evident efforts at reform, I am implying that the flaws aren't really a big deal, and neither are the moral commitments to which I am failing to live up. Returning to the "Vows" column in the New York Times, we might say that the couple's willingness to reveal the details of their messy romance and brush aside the negative effects on their families shows that they either do not recognize or do not take seriously the morally flawed beginnings of their relationship. The outrage in the comments was directed at the public revelation of their situation, on the grounds that it expressed a devaluation of marriage and parenting, disrespect for their former spouses, and a lack of consideration for their children. The general sense was that while these things happen, no one should seek to advertise it in the Times.

When discussing violations of duties to ourselves, Kant often talks in terms of debasing ourselves, lowering ourselves, or acting in a way characteristic of animals. In the case of drunkenness, Kant suggests that we bring ourselves below the level of animals. The idea seems to be that when we get drunk, we deliberately stunt our rational capacities, which is a worse state than lacking those capacities in the first place.[16] This debasement happens whether or not we have an audience; it is possible for me to behave in a degrading way even when there is no one else around to witness it. And yet, although Kant doesn't make this explicit, there is something about debasing myself in public that might well warrant outrage on the part of other people. For in presenting myself in a degrading fashion I am, on Kant's view, degrading humanity as such:

> A drunkard does no harm to another, and if he has a strong constitution he does no harm to himself, yet he is an object of contempt. We are not indifferent to cringing servility; man should not cringe and fawn; by doing so he degrades his person and loses his manhood. If a man for gain or profit submits to all indignities and makes himself the plaything of another, he casts away the worth of his manhood. Again, a lie is more a violation of one's duty to oneself than of one's duty to others. A liar, even though by his lies he does not harm to any one, yet becomes an object of contempt, he throws away his personality.[17]

If I deliberately devalue my own humanity, I express the view that humanity itself is not especially important. My lack of self-respect implies that I do not take seriously my own dignity and hence, the dignity that is the basis for respecting others. By putting my flaws on display, I am lowering the standards for everyone. So for Kant, getting drunk is a violation of a duty to myself, but posting on Facebook pictures of myself when I am drunk is a violation of a duty to all of humanity.

The rules of polite behavior require that I do my best to cover up the worst impulses of my nature. They ask me to behave courteously to people I find annoying, help people whether or not I feel like it, express gratitude for favors that I didn't much want, and act pleased when things go well for people I can't stand. These behaviors do not reflect my actual attitudes; rather, they reflect the attitudes of what we might call my "better self," the self I should be. In acting like this better self, I express my commitment to my own self-improvement and to the dignity of humanity itself.

My ability to maintain this polite public face, like my ability to maintain my front as an accomplished hostess, depends on the cooperation of other people, particularly when the cracks in my front show through. Just as tact requires that a guest pretend not to notice the clutter falling out of the coat closet when it's opened, so it also requires that others not call me out on my forced expressions of joy or gratitude. This may mean treating me as being grateful when I say that I am, even when the ambivalence in my voice is obvious. It is a collusion that expresses our joint commitment to the underlying moral principles of manners. We should feel grateful when someone tries to do something nice for us, and the rules of etiquette reflect this. If I follow the rules when I am not actually feeling grateful, I am still expressing my commitment to the principle behind those rules. And when others accept my forced expressions of gratitude as being genuine, they acknowledge my commitment to that principle.

Of course this works both ways: when I am in the audience, my part in the joint undertaking is to sustain others in their attempts to maintain a good public face. This demands that I cultivate tact as a way of helping others maintain their moral standing. Tact may require us to ascribe the right moral commitments to people on the assumption that they do have them, despite evidence to the contrary. It directs us to overlook small mistakes when possible and help provide a charitable gloss when ignoring them is not an option. As Kant puts it, it is a duty of virtue to "throw the veil of love" over the faults of other people.[18]

Adopting a public face in which we make an effort to hide our flaws, I have suggested, makes possible a form of social life in which we can act as our "best selves," even when we don't actually feel that way. It seems like a constraint, but in fact it is a way of liberating us from the worst aspects of our natures. If I can present a front of gratitude when I am not in fact feeling grateful, and if I can count on my front being accepted by my audience, then I have a way of acting on my moral commitments despite my own personal moral failings.

When I am polite to someone I dislike and he is polite to me in return, we manage to treat each other respectfully, despite our mutual dislike. Kant believed that our ability to maintain respectful relationships with people depends on our being able to engage with each other as equals. When that equality becomes unbalanced, it threatens the relationship and the associated respect. He was particularly worried about the destabilizing effects that revealing our flaws can have on our friendships:

> From a moral point of view it is, of course, a duty for one of the friends to point out the other's faults to him; this is in the other's best interests and is therefore a duty of love. But the latter sees in this a lack of the respect he expected from his friend and thinks that he has either already lost or is in constant danger of losing something of his friend's respect, since he is observed and secretly criticized by him.[19]

Of course our friends are often all too aware of our flaws, but this quote highlights something important about the way that Kant thinks about relationships. When my flaws are revealed to the world, I am vulnerable to losing their respect, particularly if I don't have similar access to their flaws.

When we behave politely to each other, we are able to engage with each other as moral equals because we are treating each other as ends. In that front region of politeness, we ignore instances of backstage behavior that, because we are only human, inevitably poke their way through. This ability to pretend not to notice things is essential to what we think of as tact. In an essay on embarrassment, Goffman describes the efforts to which we go to help others recover from their embarrassment:

> Since the individual dislikes to feel or appear embarrassed, tactful persons will avoid placing him in this position. In addition, they will often pretend not to know that he has lost composure or has grounds for losing it. They may try to suppress signs of having recognized his state or hide them behind the same kind of covering gesture that he might employ. Thus they protect his face and his feelings and presumably make it easier for him to regain composure or at least hold on to what he still has.[20]

Pretending not to notice things that would embarrass or humiliate someone else is an essential aspect of good manners, but it also has an important moral purpose. It helps maintain the other's standing as a moral equal and contributes to her self-respect.

When my dinner guests see my wildly disorganized coat closet, they get a glimpse of me when I am backstage, not trying to impress anyone. If the dinner guest is my dear friend, I probably won't be bothered by her seeing my closet, because I figure that she already knows what I'm like backstage and likes me anyway. But when it's someone I don't know well, or to put it in Goffman's terms, someone with whom I'm only on "front region" terms, I may feel embarrassed or even ashamed, depending on what standards for orderliness I think I ought to be maintaining. The fact that this person has seen a bit of my backstage behavior means that there is now a kind of imbalance in our relationship. He has gotten a fuller picture of who I am, without my having a similar picture in return, and it makes me vulnerable to his contempt or ridicule.

When elements of the backstage intrude into a front region, they are best ignored if possible. But sometimes, like in the case of the woman from Chapter 3 with the guacamole–dress problem, or my exploding closet, it cannot be ignored. A tactful guest will then respond by entering into the back region himself by revealing a similar flaw of his own, perhaps joking about the state of his own closets. This is why it is so effective to console embarrassed people with stories about one's own embarrassing moments. It restores their self-respect by returning them to the status of moral equality. Self-deprecation is a powerful social and moral tool, more so than is often recognized.

The idea that movement between front and back regions can produce problems about respect also explains why reality television (and its predecessor, the daytime talk show) has the potential to be so degrading. What makes reality television entertaining is the disparity in the position between the viewer and the participant. The viewer sees into the life of another without having to offer any kind of reciprocal window into her own life. It is a kind of socially sanctioned voyeurism. Of course only people who behave badly actually manage to get onto television. What we get, then, is a picture of people engaging in "behind the shutters" or backstage behavior with absolutely no corresponding obligation on our part to do anything to return them to a state of moral equality. Indeed, the success of reality television *depends* on our being able to look down on people, and the more they act backstage, the easier it is to feel superior to them. Not that this is the only way to respond to reality television stars—some shows take extra care to make at least some of their characters seem likeable. And some viewers do take themselves to be in a kind of moral relationship with the people they are watching on TV, perhaps by cringing on someone's behalf when she messes up on *Dancing with the Stars* or *American Idol*. But for every Susan Boyle on television, there are hundreds of others who are there primarily so that we can mock them (or watch someone else mock them), or at least feel superior to them. And this, for Kant, is a morally dangerous habit.

Social networking tools, like face-to-face encounters, can be used in the service of maintaining moral equality, and they can also be used to destroy it. Generally speaking, anonymity loosens inhibitions in the wrong direction; it frees people to say whatever they want without regard to the effects on moral relationships. Facebook, of course, is not an anonymous network, and so circumvents at least some of the problems that anonymous sites produce. But even non-anonymous online behavior follows its own set of social rules. Notably, our online revelations are affected by what psychologists call "online disinhibition," meaning that we reveal online what we would not reveal in face-to-face encounters.[21] It is not always harmful, of course. Revealing personal information can be liberating and is an essential step in intimacy. And not everyone does reveal personal information online. In the Kantian framework through which I have been arguing, the relevant question is whether the online interaction furthers the aim of a respectful moral community, or whether it undermines it. Does what we post enhance our dignity or that of other people, or does it detract from it by exposing us to the contempt of others or expressing contempt for them?

People often wonder whether we need new systems of etiquette in order to cope with online social life. Some aspects of it, granted, are different enough to warrant some rethinking. For instance, I think that our idea about who counts as a conversational partner may be evolving so as to include people who are "present" via text message or instant message. (We already, I take it, count people in when they are participating through Skype or other video communication.) It's true that online communications are instant, traceable, and devoid of important social cues on which we rely during face-to-face interactions, such as tone of voice and facial expression. But then, letters and phone calls suffer from some of the same defects. The problem of providing personal information over Twitter is not all that different than the problem of providing personal information on a postcard sent through the mail, or, for that matter, over an old-fashioned party telephone line.

Media environments like Facebook and Twitter have been criticized for their one-sidedness and potential for encouraging narcissism, certainly an important moral consideration. What reason do I have for thinking that the world is interested in my tweets, particularly when I have nothing more exciting to report than that the line at the deli is especially long today? Many tweets and status updates are so boring that they make conversations about new radio purchases seem positively enthralling by comparison, Dorothy Parker's concerns notwithstanding. On the other hand, social networking sites can help us build and maintain connections with people we care about, but don't often see. They encourage, sometimes in very peculiar ways, interesting conversations among people who might never otherwise meet in real life. In this way, they certainly contribute to moral communities, both off- and online.

In this chapter, I have argued that there is at least some moral value in being reserved about our flaws and our failings. The value lies in the fact that my effort to put on a good public face shows a commitment to morality and to my own status as an equal member of the moral community. When others accept my public face without challenging it and help me sustain it, they promote my self-respect and my ability to engage with them respectfully. My argument assumes that it is a kind of mutual pretense, rather than a one-sided deception. This is important, because as we will see in the next chapter, for all Kant's support of reserve, he is about as opposed to deliberate deception as any philosopher could be.

Polite Lies
Five

> Someone who knows too much finds it hard not to lie.[1]
>
> Ludwig Wittgenstein

If we were to ask people to list what they take to be the most important moral virtues, honesty is likely to be close to the top of most lists. After all, "Thou shalt not lie" is among the best known of the Ten Commandments. Abraham Lincoln's nickname was "Honest Abe," and of course, every American child knows the story of young George Washington telling the truth to his father about having cut down the cherry tree. Ironically, the story itself is likely not true. Even so, it remains a legend with tremendous power in American culture, which prides itself on its straight-talking style and valorizes people for their willingness to speak truthfully regardless of personal cost. Most of us probably think of ourselves as being honest, and we tend to demand honesty from other people as something to which we have a right, or at least a strong presumption.

As it turns out, however, when it comes to honesty we don't exactly practice what we preach. Social scientists who study deception have concluded that on average, we lie at least several times a day, and perhaps considerably more often than that, depending on whether we count misleading facial expressions, gestures, and the like.[2] What does this show? That we don't actually value honesty after all?

Or perhaps it shows that we value honesty, but don't actually live up to our ideals about it. This phenomenon, which ancient

Greek philosophers called *akrasia*, or weakness of will, is a familiar one to all of us.[3] Someone who is weak-willed acts contrary to her sincere beliefs about what she should do. We are weak-willed when we eat more than we know we should, get in the last word when we are aware that we should keep our mouths shut, procrastinate instead of grading student papers, and so forth. It might prove to be the case that perfect honesty is just too difficult, and most of us aren't able to live up to that standard. We lie not because we think it's all right, but because we are too cowardly or lazy to tell the truth. On this view, lying is always wrong; the problem lies with us.

No doubt weakness of will explains quite a bit of our tendencies to stretch the truth, but it can't be the entire picture. Certainly lying is sometimes taking the easy way out. If I lie to you about how your car got scratched up when I borrowed it, I don't have to face your criticism for being irresponsible or for being a bad driver. I can just blame some anonymous other driver. That being said, there do seem to be occasions when lying actually seems to be better, even morally better, than telling the truth, such as when Aunt Gladys asks me what I think of her (hideous) new hat. Usually, this is because we judge that the lie would benefit someone else, either the person to whom we are lying or else a third party. If I tell Aunt Gladys that her hat is lovely, I will make her happy; if I tell her the truth, I will hurt her feelings. We often call lies like this "white" lies, implying that that they are harmless or maybe even good.

Intuitively, it seems as though at least some white lies can be justified, or perhaps even required as a matter of politeness. Aunt Gladys already owns the hat, after all, and presumably she bought it because she liked it herself. Maybe she shouldn't have asked me what I thought of it, but given that she did, what good would it do for me to tell her the truth? A small lie here hurts no one and makes my elderly aunt happy—surely a win-win situation.

In Chapter 2, I argued that the rules of etiquette are derived from principles of morality. If it's true that morality forbids lying, then it's hard to see how polite lies could possibly be justified in the name of etiquette. Or to put it differently, if honesty is really a virtue, then wouldn't a truly virtuous person always refuse to tell a polite lie? If so, then it seems as though we might have to choose between being honest and being polite. Or maybe not. Whether a commitment to honesty is compatible with telling polite lies depends on how we think about what honesty is and how it relates to other important moral aims, like kindness and respect. We also need to look more closely at the very concept of a lie, as it is much less straightforward than it might seem on the surface.

Most etiquette books tiptoe around the subject of the polite lie, trying to give some sanction to polite lies while still condemning dishonesty in general. This distinction is nicely illustrated in Llewellyn Miller's 1967 *Encyclopedia of Etiquette*:

> Lying is a moral issue—a matter between the liar and his conscience . . . There is no easy solution for dealing with the chronic liar except to stay as far away from him as possible. . . . The social fib is, of course, a different matter. Life for all of us would be impossible without certain kindly evasions of the whole hard truth on many occasions—the empty "I'm so sorry," for example, preceding "I've just made other plans for that evening" when refusing an invitation to dinner (even though the "other plans" are to stay at home with a good book.)[4]

The 1948 edition of *Vogue's Book of Etiquette*, written by Millicent Fenwick, takes up the question in the context of teaching children to be polite, but draws a similar line:

> To the pitiless logic of a child's mind, tact is an incomprehensible compromise with truth: "If I thought the party was

horrid, shouldn't I say so, when she asked me?" But the child whose mother really cares about both truth and kindness will learn very quickly to avoid the unpleasant truth and search for a pleasant one . . . It is impossible to teach very young children that the real betrayal in human relationships is to give lies in return for truth; but in casual relations with strangers, one is not usually on a plane where absolute truths are involved.[5]

Both authors stop short of recommending outright lies, but they do evidently recognize the fact that truthful answers are not always the most polite ones

Fenwick identifies this ability to finesse the truth as tactfulness, which is widely accepted to be an important social virtue. As I discussed in the last chapter, Goffman believes that it is essential to successful social interactions, since the tact of other people is what enables all of us to sustain our public faces or fronts. Emily Post devotes an entire section of her etiquette book to the subject of tactfulness, claiming that "at least half the rules of etiquette are maxims in tact."[6] Tact, she thinks, is a combination of basic kindness and a cultivated skill of being sensitive to the feelings of others and acting in a way that will neither hurt nor humiliate them.

As we saw in the last chapter, Post acknowledges the potential for tension between tactfulness and sincerity, recognizing that a person's tactfulness can prevent others from knowing whether he is sincere. Post herself clearly placed a high value on both tact and truthfulness. Perhaps because of this, she expresses considerable confidence that it is always possible to be both tactful and truthful, even as she points out how difficult this is in practice. In support of truthfulness, Post is adamant that tact does not simply mean telling people what they want to hear: "But don't make the mistake of thinking that tact means veering like a weather vane with each breeze that blows. It means trying to cultivate the habit of paying attention and making the effort to find the pleasant or the encouraging side of truth."[7] Post's suggestion seems to be that genuine tactfulness does not require outright lies. Kind, skillful people will always find something to say that is both true and reassuring.[8]

But is Post right that a sufficiently skillful person will be able to navigate social life without ever actually telling a lie? Or are there situations where it is just impossible to be kind or respectful without misrepresenting the truth to someone? If that is the case, what does etiquette, properly informed by moral principles, direct us to do?

In order to answer this question, we need to consider just what it is that is supposed to make lying wrong in the first place, and whether the wrongness extends to every kind of lie. It matters quite a lot whether the underlying moral principle is "It's always wrong to lie" or something more nuanced, like, "It's always wrong to lie unless lying is the only way to prevent harm or pain to someone." The first version of the principle probably would not sanction polite lies, but the second version might. So let us consider what can be said on behalf of these principles.

The general question of whether lying can ever be morally permissible is one that has interested philosophers for quite some time. In The Republic, Plato argued on behalf of what he called a "noble lie" aimed at benefiting those to whom it is told. The noble lie consists in telling people that they have gold, silver, or iron in their souls, with the aim of structuring society in such a way that each member would be content with his or her role. (People with gold souls would, of course, be the rulers, whereas the people with iron souls would be the workers.) It's not clear just how serious Plato was about this idea, but it has been influential. Aldous Huxley's dystopian novel, Brave New World, is largely an instantiation of Plato's noble lie in a technologically sophisticated world, although in this case, individuals have been both engineered and conditioned to accept their social positions. Uncomfortable questions or expressions of doubt are met not with honest responses, but with soma, a mysterious drug that spins a pleasant haze over everything.

Most people, including Huxley, would reject the claim that it's a good idea to purchase happiness at the expense of truth. Popular films like *The Matrix* and *The Truman Show* reinforce this view. Truman, after all, chooses to leave his perfectly tranquil televised life behind in favor of leading a more honest, authentic existence. And yet, although we are good at proclaiming the value of truth, we are less good at saying what is so valuable about it. What purpose does truthfulness serve in our society? Why does it matter whether we are willing to speak the truth to others and face the truth ourselves, like Truman chooses to do?

One obvious point in favor of telling the truth to people is the idea that in lying, we wrong the person to whom we are telling the lie. The argument that we have a duty to others not to lie to them and they have a corresponding right to truth from us was made quite thoroughly by the seventeenth-century Dutch philosopher Hugo Grotius. Grotius argued that in joining together into society, we enter into a tacit agreement with others to be truthful when we speak. This is because "without such an obligation the invention of speech would have been void of result."[9] Grotius thinks that this gives other people a right to expect us to speak truthfully. It is a right that can be waived or set aside by joint agreement, but it is nevertheless a right. Thus, if I speak falsely to someone who has not agreed to give up his right to truth from me, I violate a duty toward him.

Kant developed a similar line of thought as part of what has proven to be one of the most impassioned arguments against lying that any philosopher has ever given. Kant seems to have taken the view that lying is always and everywhere wrong, no matter what the reason or what harm will befall someone if we tell the truth.[10] The argument itself is multi-layered, but at its center is his idea, discussed in Chapter 1, that we are morally required to treat ourselves and others as ends. He claims that lying to someone is a violation of a duty of respect that we owe him or her as a rational being.

Recall that on Kant's view, we are both rationally and morally committed to treating people as beings with dignity and unconditional value. Suppose I tell someone a lie because I want her to choose a course of action or agree to something that, if she knew the truth, she would not. By lying to her, I cause her to have an inaccurate picture of the situation, thereby constraining her ability to act in a fully rational way. I may do this by accident if I tell her something false by mistake, but when I lie, I do so deliberately. I thus treat her as an object that I can manipulate for my own purposes, rather than as a rational being with the right to make her own decisions. This is the sense in which Kant thinks that lying to someone violates a duty to treat her as an end in herself.

Kant believed that lies are always a violation of self-respect as well. His idea seems to be that there is something especially underhanded about lying. Resorting to a lie is a degrading way of achieving my ends. In this way, it resembles hitting someone from behind—the other person cannot see it coming and cannot defend herself, which is what makes it unfair. Lying perverts what Kant took to be the natural purpose of speech and conversation, using them for something entirely different. This is why Kant thought that lying is a worse kind of debasement than something like gluttony or satisfying lust. In overeating or seeking out sexual gratification, I behave like an animal. In lying, I behave worse than an animal because I am abusing rationality.

Kant's stand against lying is uncompromising, to put it mildly. In an infamous exchange with a fellow scholar named Benjamin Constant, Kant went so far as to assert that it would be wrong to lie to someone who comes to the door asking you to reveal the whereabouts of some innocent third party, whom he intends to murder. Few people would say that it would be wrong to lie in such circumstances, but Kant apparently takes a hard line here. You cannot lie, even to a would-be murderer at the door.[11]

Importantly, however, this is not because in lying to the would-be murderer, we treat him disrespectfully. While in general, people have a right against us that we not manipulate them through the use of lies, this does not straightforwardly apply to people who are attempting to extract information from us unjustly.[12] Someone bent on murder is, on Kant's view, necessarily bent on a course of action that is both immoral and irrational. Might this give us some justification for interfering with his plan? Let's suppose that the would-be murderer is only temporarily irrational, and that in an hour he will be rational again. Could it actually be more respectful to prevent him from acting in a way he will regret? If so, then perhaps lying to the murderer is actually a way of treating him as an end. Perhaps we respect him by responding to him in the way that we presume he would want us to respond if he were rational.

There is, I think, room in Kant's theory to say this about the murderer at the door, although it would be a very controversial reading of the theory and Kant himself probably would have rejected it. But we are not yet through Kant's reasons for thinking lying is wrong. What he actually says about the murderer case is not that it is wrong because it violates a duty to the murderer, but because it violates a duty we owe to all humanity. It is this duty that is most relevant to the permissibility of polite lies, so I will discuss it in some detail.

Kant believed that it is a deep truth about human beings that we desire knowledge, and also that our quest for this knowledge is limited by our own inexperience. We are thus heavily reliant on the word of others in order for us to fulfill our rational desire to increase our own knowledge of the world. For instance, I cannot myself travel to every country in the world; in order to have knowledge about the countries I have not visited, I must depend on the veracity of people who have been there and who are reporting back. They, in turn, are depending on my veracity about my experiences. The fact that we are dependent on each other in this way generates a mutual obligation to be honest in our communications with each other.

This suggests that the virtue of honesty is in part a kind of civic duty, something that we owe to our fellow community members on the grounds that society itself couldn't function without it. Certainly this is the idea behind, say, taking oaths of office or oaths in court or before Congress. If I lie in court, I obstruct the judicial process itself. The oath is a way of requiring me to state publicly that I will live up to my duty as a citizen to contribute to the smooth, fair, and just functioning of that process. Some have also argued that truthfulness is a religious duty that we owe to God. The fact that many of our public oaths are sworn on a Bible emphasizes that the duty to truthfulness is a duty on a grand scale. Of course, some people take that to mean that it is only when we are swearing on a Bible that we really have to tell the truth. St. Augustine, who was one of history's more vociferous opponents of lying, made a point of rejecting such reasoning. On his view, we lie whenever what we say is at odds with what we believe in our hearts to be true. Augustine argued that the wrongness of lying has to do with that relationship, not with the effects of the lie.[13]

The importance of honesty in maintaining and sustaining a strong community is perhaps most evident in its absence. Societies marked by massive distrust, whether of the government or of their fellow citizens, are societies that quickly dissolve into war and other forms of violence. Truth, after all, is essential to trust, and trust is essential to moral community. In the efforts to heal South Africa after the ravages of apartheid, the Truth and Reconciliation Commission played a central role in bringing human rights violations to light and facilitating reconciliation and restoration. The idea behind that Commission was that it was necessary to be truthful about what had happened so as to establish trust and begin to rebuild a functioning community.

Neither Kant nor Constant gives us very much information about the context in which the would-be murderer is making the request. There's good reason to think that Kant, at least, regarded the person as some kind of state official with a legal and perhaps moral right to demand an answer about the person's where-abouts.[14] (Kant explicitly assumes that the person must be given an answer, that remaining silent or tackling the would-be murderer is not an option.) If so, then it would be a very unusual circumstance, but not unprecedented. Modern day critics of Kant often wonder whether he would say the same about lying to Nazis who knock at the door and demand to know whether Jews are hidden in the house. It's hard to believe that we could have any kind of duty to tell the truth in those circumstances. Indeed, the opposite seems to be true. If anything, there would be a duty to lie to protect the Jewish fugitives.

St. Thomas Aquinas, the thirteenth-century Dominican priest, theologian, and philosopher, divided lies into three categories: useful, jocular, and harmful.[15] Useful lies are aimed at benefiting someone or preventing her from being harmed. Jocular lies are told in the spirit of fun or creating pleasure, like a tall tale or a joke. Harmful lies aim at harming someone or profiting the one who tells them. Aquinas thinks that the moral analysis of a lie depends greatly on what kind of lie it is, since the justification for a lie depends in part on its end. Useful and jocular lies aim at good ends, whereas harmful lies aim at evil ends. Aquinas does not necessarily condone useful or jocular lies, but he does not think that they can be put on the same plane as harmful lies, which he regards as evidencing a much greater level of sinfulness.[16] By this reasoning, it's possible that the lie to the Nazi can be justified, both because it aims at another's good and averts an evil and also because Aquinas probably would not have regarded the Nazi soldiers as having any kind of legitimate authority in the first place.

Aquinas separates lies by their aims, not their effects. Utilitarians like John Stuart Mill, by contrast, would distinguish permissible and impermissible lies by whether or not they produce the best outcome. A lie is justified if and only if it maximizes happiness, meaning that it produces the greatest benefit for the greatest number of people. Lying to Nazis probably upsets the Nazis, but certainly benefits everyone else and so would be justified according to utilitarianism.

Telling a lie to a Nazi at the door is not exactly a classic example of a white lie, since the stakes are very high and we tend to think of white lies as being about trivial matters. But lies to potential murderers and lies to people who have just gotten bad haircuts or who have invited us to boring parties have in common the fact that they are aimed at benefiting someone else, or at least preventing harm. This is what makes white lies seem harmless, if not actually good. The harm being prevented by lying to Nazis is, of course, a much greater harm than the hurt feelings that would be produced by someone's truthful opinion of a haircut. But they are both harms, and if a lie prevents them without creating offsetting harms, then the lie would be right by utilitarian standards. This is a point of quite fundamental disagreement between Kantians and utilitarians.

The question of whether a polite lie can be justified is further complicated by the fact that it is not entirely clear how we should even determine what counts as a lie. Defining a lie turns out to be a surprisingly complicated issue. We might think that it would be straightforward to define a lie as a false statement. But just a little bit of reflection will show that this will not do. For one thing, we sometimes say things that are false, believing that they are true. Suppose you have told me that you are going straight home after our meeting. Later that afternoon, Caroline asks me where you are, and I say that you have gone home. But unbeknownst to me, you decided on a whim to take in the latest Harry Potter movie. So you are not in fact at home; you are at the movie theater. My statement that you are at home is false, but I have not lied to Caroline. I am simply mistaken. Lying, it seems, requires at least some intent to deceive.[17]

The fact that the intent to deceive is important explains why we may feel inclined to say that it's possible to lie without saying a word. Suppose that I am again hosting a dinner party. I am a lousy cook, but I don't want my dinner guests to know. So I order a mouthwatering selection of foods from a local restaurant, bring them home, and put them into my own baking and serving dishes. I leave some gourmet cookbooks on the counter and perhaps even go so far as to splatter small bits of sauce on my sink and backsplash. My guests, quite naturally, arrive at the belief that I have cooked the meal, but luckily for me, none of them ask me that question directly. When they compliment me on the meal, I simply smile and thank them. Notice that I can do all this without ever saying anything false. And yet, it's clearly deceptive in the same way that deliberately false statements are deceptive. If there's a moral difference between this scenario and another one where I explicitly say that I cooked the food, it doesn't seem to be a significant one.

So not all false statements are lies, because we are sometimes mistaken about the facts, and some behavior is just as deceptive as a spoken lie, even though no words are said. It is the intention that seems most relevant. What this means is that the definition of a lie needs to be narrowed in one direction and perhaps broadened in another. We need to narrow the category of lies so as to exclude mistakes, and we may also want to broaden it to include forms of deception that do not involve any statements at all.[18]

Complicating matters still further is the fact that even statements known to be false don't always seem to count as lies. Consider, for instance, the following letter to Miss Manners:

Dear Miss Manners: One cannot walk the streets of any big city without passing a beggar who intones, "Can you spare some change?" or who simply rattles some coins in a plastic cup. I usually avert my eyes and try to ignore him, but that response denies the undeniable. The beggar is a person, and as such, he surely deserves, at a minimum, an acknowledgment of his existence. In an effort to exhibit a semblance of humanity, I sometimes make eye contact and state simply, "Sorry, no." But that is not really acceptable either. First, the answer is usually a lie, and second, the line is usually uttered with a measure of impatience or condescension that degrades us both. Is there any response that can uphold the dignity of both participants? Or is the encounter so inherently undignified that one should escape as quickly and quietly as possible?[19]

This letter nicely illustrates the ways in which etiquette problems tend to have many different moral layers. The writer is clearly uncomfortable with lying to the person asking for money, and he or she is also sensitive to how social inequality affects encounters between strangers. Martin agrees that the inequality problem is a difficult one to solve, but she dispatches with the honesty problem quickly:

> "Can you spare some change?" is an idiomatic expression meaning "Will you give me some change?" rather than an inquiry into the amount of your disposable income. Thus, "Sorry, no," or better yet, the briefer "Sorry," is a reasonable and polite answer.[20]

Martin is here making a point that we can all recognize from our own experiences, which is that not all the conventions of conversation that we employ are meant to be taken literally. Of course, the person asking for change is likely counting on the fact that the passer-by can in fact spare some change and that the honest ones will react as the letter-writer did. The rhetorical force of "Can you spare some change?" is different and more compelling than the force of "Will you give me some change?"

But the wording of the request does not change its substance. This is why passers-by are justified in responding to the substance of the request, even when it doesn't exactly match the wording. The word "No" is not a truthful response to the question "Can you spare some change?" It is, however, a truthful response to the question, "Will you give me some change?" So if the letter-writer is answering the latter question, she is not being dishonest.

This is even more obvious in the American convention of greeting people with questions like, "How are you?" or "How's it going?" or "What's up?" These are not normally meant to be genuine inquiries into the other person's life, which is why they are normally best answered with something along the lines of "Fine, and you?" or "Not much, what about you?" The answer is just as much of a platitude. The person with the bad cold still claims to be fine, and the parent in the parking lot trying to corral four small children into their car seats still says that she's not doing much. Of course, it's possible to ask how someone is and really want to know the answer, but in that case, we need to convey the fact that it's a genuine question by employing a different tone of voice ("How *are* you?") or a gesture (a hand on the shoulder).

This is all quite important because at least some of the lies that we tend to think of as white lies probably aren't really lies in the first place. In the quotation from The Encyclopedia of Etiquette at the beginning of the chapter, the statement that one has other plans for the evening is not a lie. This is part because it's true (if it's true that one has made plans to read a book, then the statement is true, even if the plans have been made seconds before the statement is uttered). But it is also because vague statements attached to refusals of invitations are generally understood not to be literal accounts of one's alternate plans. The deceptiveness of a statement seems to depend not just on what the speaker says, but also on what the speaker intends or expects the hearer to believe.

Children sometimes think that they can tell a lie without doing something wrong if they cross their fingers behind their back. The idea, I suppose, is that crossing your fingers somehow reverses what philosophers call the "truth-value" of a statement, turning something false into something true. Most adults would reject this as silly, and certainly not effective in rendering a statement true or permissible. Of course if the hearer knows that the speaker is crossing her fingers, then she's not likely to be deceived by the statement. But merely crossing one's fingers does not change either the fact that the statement is a lie or the wrongness of telling it. The other person is just as deceived as she would be without the finger-crossing.

Although we reject crossed fingers as a defense against the charge of lying, there is a long tradition of defending something not too far removed from it. This is the practice of "mental reservation" (or "reservatio mentis" for those who think that justifications sound better in Latin). The idea behind a mental reservation is that one says only part of one's thought out loud, finishing or qualifying the statement in one's head. The entire statement, including the part in one's head, is true, but the part that is said out loud is false when taken by itself.

If Kant is right, the moral problem with lying is primarily located in the intent to deceive. False statements like "I'm fine" generally aren't meant to deceive, and so wouldn't violate his prohibition against lying. But if I say only half of a statement out loud, saying the rest in my head, I do intend to deceive the other person, since I intend that he believe half my statement in ignorance of the rest. Let's suppose that I say the following out loud to the person issuing an invitation to a party I know will be horrible: "Oh, I'm sure everyone will enjoy themselves . . ." I then say in my head (the mental reservation) ". . . more than they would if they were getting root canals without Novocain." The entire statement might be true, but I clearly intend to deceive the party-thrower by saying only the first half out loud.

Unsurprisingly, Kant rejects the idea that mental reservation could be a defense against the charge of deliberate deception.[21]

When it comes to polite lies, then, the Kantian position will have to be that if we are presenting what we say as being true, and if we expect that our listener will reasonably expect us to be speaking the truth, we are under an obligation to speak the truth. These conditions are not always in place. If my friend asks me whether I like her new haircut, she may or may not be asking me to tell the truth. Sometimes such requests are simply requests for validation. When that is the case, I do not deceive my friend by giving her a comforting answer.

It is worth noting how important conventions of language are when it comes to gauging whether someone is either requesting or offering a truthful opinion. Knowing what is being requested and what is expected requires sensitivity to nuance, but it also requires knowledge of particular conventions of speech, like how words like "really" are used in ordinary conversation. "Tell me what you think" is not always the same as "Tell me what you really think," which is also not always the same as "Tell me what you *really* think." No doubt people asking for opinions need to be very careful in how they phrase their requests.

If, however, my friend does genuinely want a truthful answer, then on Kant's view, any answer I give her must be truthful. This is because it would be presumptuous of me to decide unilaterally that I know better than my friend what she should and should not hear about herself. If I say what is false with the hope that she will believe it is true, I treat her disrespectfully because I am failing to treat her as a fully rational agent. Instead, I treat her as I would treat a child or someone who is not fully up to the task of dealing with reality. My attempts at protecting her feelings are, in this case, patronizing.

Now as we saw in Chapter 4, Kant doesn't think we are required to give answers whenever we are asked questions. We can maintain silence, or we can change the subject to something else. Of course in practice this basically amounts to giving a truthful answer. If my friend asks me if I like her new haircut and I don't say anything at all, or I start talking about the possibility of rain, then she will undoubtedly catch on and infer that I do not like her haircut. So just saying that we don't need to give an answer doesn't really help us out all that much.

What we need, of course, is the skill of tact, which enables us to respond to questions truthfully without saying anything hurtful. Emily Post, who shares Kant's objections to deliberate deception, says the following:

> Let us say you go to see a friend who has just refurnished her house. You think she has spoiled it completely. And WHAT do you say? You can only distress your friend if you tell her, "Well, I think the room is hideous." It's finished; she has to live in it, and criticism would be wanton rudeness! On the other hand, if she had told you about it before redoing it, you would have been lacking in interest not to give her your thoughtful opinion. Which again doesn't mean tearing the whole plan to pieces merely to display your own cleverness . . .[22]

Undoubtedly Post is right that a tactful person would not say that the room is hideous after it is finished. Although she doesn't give examples of a more tactful answer, we can probably come up with our own ideas: "That's a really bold color scheme" or, "I especially like that lamp over in the corner." Post herself says that tact involves "paying attention and making the effort to find the pleasant or encouraging side of the truth."[23] Presumably Kant would sanction tact understood this way. I say nothing false, so I treat the person respectfully, but I am also mindful of the negative effects that unnecessarily cutting or sarcastic remarks can have. To put it slightly differently, I should say only what is true, but I should choose carefully which true things I say, and I should say them nicely.

Utilitarians are likely to think of these concerns about saying only what is true as much ado about nothing. Recall that on the utilitarian account, a lie is justified if it maximizes happiness. On this view, Truman's decision to leave the set of The Truman Show may prove to have been a mistake if, as is certainly possible, the world outside proves crueler than the world he left. There's no inherent value in living more truthfully; the life that is a lie might just prove to be the happier one. (Utilitarians, however, would take into account not just Truman's own happiness, but also the happiness of the other actors on the show and the millions of fans with a personal investment in how Truman's life turns out.) The average utilitarian is not going to lose sleep over a white lie to Aunt Gladys about her hat. Telling such lies is probably a happiness-maximizing thing to do, and if it is, then they are not just morally permissible, but morally good. The same is true in spades for telling lies to Nazis and other would-be murderers at the door. For utilitarians, it's patently obvious that lies in such cases are morally justified.

When it comes to lies that are told to ill-intentioned people for the benefit of innocent third parties, it's hard to argue with the utilitarian conclusion. Recall that even Kant agreed that lying to a murderer at the door isn't a violation of a duty to the murderer. It's a violation of our duty to humanity as such, and it could conceivably be argued that no such duty holds in a world ruled by Nazis. In general, Kant thought that even if the world is crashing down around me, I still have to hold up my little corner of the moral universe to the best of my ability. There is something noble about this, but there is also something noble in the act of protecting innocent people from the murderous intentions of others. Of course, very few of our white lies involve this level of heroism and when they do, the question of whether the lie is polite or not seems largely beside the point. The more controversial cases for etiquette are those in which the lie is told for some much less weighty reason, such as not wanting to hurt someone's feelings.

Kant is committed to the idea that lying to spare someone's feelings is not actually a benefit to that person. He doesn't say that in so many words, but it is implicit in his account. My lie to Aunt Gladys about her hat may seem kind, but if she really wants my honest opinion, then I am not benefiting her by hiding it from her. Kindness must be constrained by respect, for Kant, if it is really to be a benefit to her. If she wants my honest opinion about something that she has done, then by lying to her, I am denying her access to something she wants and perhaps even needs in order to know herself better. Lying may spare her temporary pain, but it blocks important avenues for her to develop self-knowledge or knowledge about the world.

What about lies that are told not to spare someone's feelings, but to preserve her self-respect? Recall that in Chapter 4, I argued that we have moral reason to cooperate with others in their attempts to present a certain kind of front. I said that preserving another's front can mean accepting an apology or an expression of gratitude at face value, even when we know that it is being offered grudgingly. It can also mean, as Kant says, "throwing the veil" over other people's faults, so as to encourage mutual charity and respect. In practice, this may mean that I need to resort to not-entirely-honest methods for helping others preserve their fronts. I may need to pretend that I did not see what I did, or at least provide assurance that others did not. I may need to engage in exaggerated self-deprecation in order to restore someone's moral equality or present a slightly altered picture of reality. ("Really, *everyone* puts his foot in his mouth at least once during a job interview.") Probably it is possible to engage in such front-preserving behavior without telling absolute untruths, but there is no question that it requires considerable tact. People who have the skill to preserve someone's self-respect without saying anything false should undoubtedly do so. A more difficult question is whether people who don't quite have that level of tact should lie to preserve someone else's public standing. If I really can't find the pleasant side of the truth, should I say something false or should I remain silent?

Much of the time, we recognize it when others are attempting to help us save face. In such cases, we might not take what they say to be the literal truth anyway. The pretense involved with sustaining another's front is in many ways cooperative. Thus, if I do something really embarrassing and my friend claims that she didn't notice, I may know that she did in fact notice. In such cases, her statement that she didn't notice is more like a statement that she is planning to act as if she didn't notice. If so, it is not, strictly speaking, a lie.

Kant would surely say that there are limits to how far I should go to preserve someone's self-respect, just as there are limits to how far I should go to preserve her feelings. Those limits, for Kant, are generally also based in respect. As we discussed earlier, attempts to shield a person's feelings can be patronizing. So can attempts to preserve her self-respect. Consider again the use of self-deprecation as a way of restoring another's moral standing. If I have just done something really stupid, and you tell me about the time you did something equally stupid, I will probably feel better. But if I later found out that you simply made the whole thing up, I am likely to feel even worse. Self-deprecation is an effective way of restoring someone's moral standing, but only if it's truthful. Otherwise, it is counterproductive.

What about white lies told to preserve my own self-respect? Kant, like most of us, would disapprove of white lies that are told strictly to preserve myself from harm. Lying about my GPA in college may not cause anyone any real harm, and may improve others' opinion of me enough to land me a job, but Kant is surely right that there is something fundamentally dishonorable about it. Telling white lies to preserve my own self-respect, however, might seem more justifiable.

For Kant, the idea of lying for the sake of one's own self-respect would make little sense. As we saw earlier in the chapter, he held that lying is an outright violation of self-respect, remarking that "the dishonor that accompanies a lie also accompanies the liar like his shadow."[24] It is a misuse of rationality and, he thought, beneath our dignity. But that doesn't mean that we are under any obligation to reveal everything about ourselves that others want to know.

In a video of Slate.com's "Dear Prudence" feature, Emily Yoffe takes a question from someone who is trying to decide how to respond when she is asked how she and her husband met.[25] In fact, they met when she was working in a strip bar, but she doesn't want to make that part public. Yoffe advises her just to say that she was a waitress, on the grounds that it's true in a way and that a truthful answer doesn't require any details. (One wonders, though, what would happen if the questioner asked which restaurant.)

In Chapter 4, I argued that we are morally justified in hiding our flaws from others, on the grounds that doing so is a way of preserving our self-respect. Kant himself was not terribly concerned about this as a potential form of deception, since he saw it as a mutual form of pretense with some transparency built in. We all have flaws, we all know that everyone has flaws, and we all know that everyone is hiding their flaws. So it's not deceptive in the usual sense.

But there's something more we can say about polite lies in the context of moral fronts; namely, that some front-preserving false statements may not really be lies in the usual sense. By that I mean that they are a way of expressing moral ideals and sustaining moral fronts, rather than attempts to deceive people about reality. In the last chapter, I argued that a polite expression of gratitude when we are not feeling grateful expresses how we think we should feel. It may be deceptive as an actual report of my current feelings, but it is not deceptive as a report of my moral attitudes and commitments. If expressions of gratitude are always supposed to be current status reports, then there may be a problem. But there is no reason to think that they must be that way. Politely thanking someone for an awful present does not necessarily declare that I am grateful; it only declares that I believe that gratitude is the morally appropriate response to being given a gift. Or at least most of the time.

Six

We do not quite forgive a giver. The hand that feeds us is in some danger of being bitten.[1]

Ralph Waldo Emerson

In the fall of 2010, Amazon.com filed a patent for a technical innovation that would enable people to block the delivery of unwanted gifts. The technology permits potential gift recipients to set up rules that would, for instance, convert all gifts from Aunt Mildred to gift certificates, with or without Aunt Mildred's knowledge. The new system would also enable people to send thank you notes for the original gift, adding to the deceptive possibilities. Amazon, of course, has a financial interest in reducing the number of returned items it handles, which is presumably why it developed the technology. Supporters of the system also point to the environmental benefits of blocking shipments of packages that are destined to be shipped right back.

Even so, the revelation of Amazon's plans set off a minor firestorm among people who think that this new technology will destroy the last remnants of thoughtfulness and gratitude remaining in the practice of exchanging gifts. The *Washington Post* cites Anna Post, Emily Post's great-great-granddaughter, as expressing disapproval:

> "This idea totally misses the spirit of gift giving . . . The point of gift giving is to allow someone else to go through that

action of buying something for us. Otherwise, giving a gift just becomes another one of the world's transactions."[2]

Post's statement suggests that gift-giving is supposed to be markedly different from other forms of contractual exchanges. Just what is supposed to make it different, however, is not entirely clear. The giving of gifts is a practice with ancient history and many different cultural forms. It is laden with meaning, but the meanings are varied and often muddied by other factors.[3] In contemporary American culture, the ideal gift is generally thought to be one given out of motives of love and affection, chosen with exquisite care and attention to the recipient's needs, desires, and tastes. Such a gift would, ideally, be received in the spirit of grateful delight, and thanks expressed through artfully chosen words.

Of course our actual practices of gift-giving rarely live up to this ideal. If the contemporary etiquette books and columns are any indication, gift-giving in the real world is the source of considerable angst. Etiquette books written in the last several decades tend to have an entire chapter or section devoted to gift-giving. Interestingly, this is a fairly new phenomenon. The social complexities of gift-giving are barely addressed by early-to-mid-twentieth-century etiquette writers like Emily Post, Lillian Eichler, Amy Vanderbilt, and Millicent Fenwick. Perhaps gift-giving was less common back then (although most of them devote space to discussing gifts for hospital nurses) or less fraught with anxiety. Emily Post mostly concerned herself with the etiquette of giving flowers, not the etiquette of giving gift cards to the mailman. Whatever the reason, the proper way to exchange gifts is certainly a major topic in American etiquette now.

The etiquette problems associated with giving and receiving things cover a wide range. Do I need to bring a gift to my aunt's 75th birthday party, or my colleague's retirement bash, and if so, what kind of gift is appropriate? Should I try to help someone in a wheelchair across a busy intersection, or would it be demeaning her by implying that she cannot manage by herself? Do I offer my seat on the subway to an elderly man or will he be offended? Can I say anything to my friend who is dating a married man about what a terrible idea the relationship is? Do I have to thank someone when she gives me a present I find mildly offensive? What do I say to well-meaning strangers who dole out advice about how I should raise my children?

In this chapter, I will argue that these etiquette issues have something in common, namely, that they all fall under the heading of a moral principle that philosophers generally call the principle of beneficence. Obligations of beneficence, broadly speaking, are obligations to improve the lives of others. Nearly everyone agrees that beneficence is a morally good thing, but there is considerable disagreement about how important it is and how it relates to other moral obligations, such as the requirement to respect other people's privacy, choices, and tastes.

The flip side of beneficence is gratitude. Gratitude is often considered a virtue, although it doesn't fit well into traditional understandings of virtue like Aristotle's. But whether or not it really is a virtue, gratitude is certainly morally good, and perhaps even morally required on some occasions. Gratitude is a complex phenomenon, involving both a feeling and the expression of that feeling to the person toward whom we are feeling grateful. Sometimes the two come apart. We can certainly feel gratitude without expressing it, and we can (and often do) express gratitude without feeling it. Etiquette generally concerns itself with the expression of gratitude, but here we will be considering both the feeling and its outward expressions.

In this chapter, I will start with a general discussion of the principle of beneficence and its relationship to other moral aims and obligations. The opening quote from Emerson suggests that beneficence is not always gratefully received. I will examine the interaction between appropriate beneficence and appropriate gratitude as it pertains primarily to gifts, but also to favors, and advice.

One of the main philosophical debates about beneficence itself is whether it ever rises to the level of a strict obligation, by which I mean something that generates a right for someone else. I have an obligation not to steal your new iPhone, however much I might want it, and you have a right against me that I not steal it. If I violate this right, you are entitled to seek compensation and perhaps also retribution against me.

Almost by definition, gifts are not like this. No one has a right to receive a gift from me, however badly I behave in not giving one. If there were such a right, then the item in question would not be a gift. The same goes for favors and advice—if someone has a right that I do him a favor or give him advice, then the action falls into a different category.[4] Of course this doesn't stop people from demanding gifts, particularly for weddings where, at least in American society, gift-giving norms are at their strongest. This is a point on which etiquette experts are unanimous—demanding a gift is always rude. In fact, this delicacy extends even to indications that one is expecting gifts, which is why etiquette experts also generally agree that it is rude to enclose with a wedding invitation a list of stores where the couple is registered for gifts. The couple can register, and people who enquire about the registry can be answered. But the suggestion that gifts are expected or even anticipated is always rude.

Miss Manners put it this way in response to a letter asking whether it's acceptable to put "cards and gifts optional" on an invitation to an anniversary party:

> Optional as opposed to what? As opposed to "Cards and gifts are mandatory, and steps will be taken to collect from those who do not contribute?" Presents are always optional, and it is not the place of people who happen to be celebrating an anniversary, or any other occasion, to expect them—not even by attempts to discourage them.[5]

But even though presents are optional, there are occasions, such as weddings that one attends, where failing to give a present would normally be quite rude. We might not want to put it so strongly as saying that one is *obligated* to give a wedding gift, but it comes close. Anyone who attends a wedding is expected to give some kind of present.[6] Although the bridal couple cannot themselves criticize slackers without seeming greedy, the rest of us would probably be justified in thinking of them as selfish and inconsiderate.

The etiquette norms of doing favors for people resemble the norms for gift-giving in some ways, but not in others.[7] Like gifts, favors cannot normally be demanded, but they can reasonably be expected. Unlike gifts, however, they can also be requested. The person at whom the request is directed is permitted to refuse, but we generally think that a person who declines to do a favor needs to have a decent reason for declining, so long as the request for the favor is a reasonable one. (Not all such requests are, of course. Except in emergencies, it is normally considered rude to ask too big a favor, to ask for favors too frequently, or to ask strangers for anything other than a very minor favor.) Advice, unlike gifts, should normally not be bestowed without asking. This is because unsought advice can be condescending, implying that one is incapable of solving a problem or accomplishing a task on one's own. We can request advice, and when we do, there is a strong presumption that it should be given if possible. Still, as with favors and gifts, it does not seem right to think of advice as something that can be demanded as a matter of right or obligation.

The norms surrounding the exchange of gifts, favors, and advice are obviously quite complicated, and they occupy a rather murky territory in both etiquette and ethics. We can, however, shed some light on the subject by examining the moral principle that underlies the etiquette of giving and receiving; namely, the principle of beneficence. Beneficence has a robust philosophical history, and there continues to be considerable discussion about the nature and extent of our obligations to improve the situations of others or add to their pleasure. It is, of course, something that we often want to do anyway, particularly when it comes to loved ones. But it is also something that we are at least occasionally required to do. Moreover, there are moral constraints governing how we do it. As we know, gifts can be insulting, favors can be unwanted, and advice can be patronizing. From the standpoint of both etiquette and ethics, there are better and worse ways of going about helping people.

As we have seen, Kant recognized that we have a moral duty to respect other people as ends in themselves.[8] But he also believed that we have duties of love toward people, including duties of beneficence and gratitude. A person's status as an end in herself generates two different types of duties toward her— perfect and imperfect duties. Perfect duties are, for the most part, duties not to interfere with the person or the exercise of her rationality. Duties not to kill people, lie to them, or steal their iPhones are all perfect duties. Imperfect duties, by contrast, are duties to adopt ends or commitments.

Kant believed that there are two commitments that we are morally required to take on: our own perfection and the happiness of others. What it means to have my own perfection as my end is that I must commit myself to improving my moral character and also cultivating my talents, so that I will be worthy of my status as a being with dignity. Committing myself to the happiness of others requires that I take seriously their ends, projects, and goals, and help them in achieving them.

Perfect duties require perfect compliance from us. I cannot defend myself against a murder charge by pointing out that I killed only two of the five people I felt like killing this week. Imperfect duties, by contrast, permit us to exercise some latitude about how we fulfill them. I must cultivate my talents, but not every second of the day. I must also give to charity, but I don't have to give to every single charity that asks me for money. I get to choose, and while my choices must reflect a serious commitment to helping others, I cannot reasonably be criticized for devoting my efforts to, say, fighting homelessness rather than leukemia.

Perfect duties, on Kant's view, limit everything else that we do, including fulfilling imperfect duties like cultivating our talents and helping others. If I have musical talent, I should learn to play the piano, but not if it means stealing your baby grand. And I should do my best to get you the medical care you need to survive, but I cannot do it by knocking someone unconscious and taking her kidney. Whatever beneficence requires from us, it is constrained at the outset by the perfect duties that we have toward both ourselves and other people. (Thus, Kantian ethics also prohibits helping people by demeaning ourselves.)

So there is some sense in which perfect duties have priority for Kant, but he does take imperfect duties like beneficence very seriously as well. In Kant's eyes, we aren't fully respecting someone as a being with dignity if we do nothing more than refrain from killing him or stealing his stuff. Acknowledging someone's status as a rational being also means taking seriously his projects and plans and at least sometimes helping him promote or achieve them. (Kant did make an exception for immoral ends. I do not have a duty of beneficence to help you rob a bank.) If you are stranded on the side of the highway with a flat tire, I have a perfect duty to make sure I do not run you over with my car as I speed by. But while I am not strictly obligated to stop and help you change your tire, Kant thinks that my imperfect duty of beneficence toward you does always give me a reason to stop and help. I may have other important things to do, and I may be confident that someone else will stop and help you. But Kant thought that a world in which no one ever helps anyone else is a world in which we don't take the dignity of other people as seriously as we should. So at least sometimes, I should be the person who stops to help change a tire.

To summarize, Kant believed that we have both perfect and imperfect duties toward other people, with beneficence as an imperfect duty. A slightly different (and not entirely equivalent) way of putting it is to say that we have duties of both respect and love. Kant, however, recognized that the demands of respect and the demands of love can sometimes be in tension with each other:

> The principle of mutual love admonishes men constantly to *come closer* to one another; that of the respect they owe one another, to keep themselves *at a distance* from one another; and should one of these great moral forces fail, "the nothingness (immorality), with gaping throat, would drink up the whole kingdom of (moral) beings like a drop of water."[9]

Our duties of love and concern instruct us to draw closer to people and their problems, but our duties of respect toward those same people also command us to keep our distance so as not to interfere unduly with their lives. Anyone who has ever dithered about approaching a stranger crying in a public place is familiar with this tension. One wants to offer help, but one doesn't want to intrude.

Generally speaking, on Kant's view, our duty not to provide unwanted interference with people's lives is more stringent than our duty to help them. If someone doesn't want my help or my advice, I have a duty of respect toward her to back off, at least if the other person is a rational agent. (My duties to people whose rationality is immature or impaired are different. I do not have to go away just because my 5 year-old tells me I should.) Kantian beneficence demands that I promote the ends that other people actually have, not the ones that I think they should have. I may think you look wonderful in orange, but if I know that you hate the color, I should not give you an orange sweater for your birthday. To do so, Kant thinks, would be disrespectful. It suggests that I know what's best for you and you do not. Like white lies, gifts of this sort are patronizing, as far as Kant is concerned. Even if I know that I can help you make your computer's memory more efficient or your office more organized, I ought not simply sweep in and do it for you unless you've given me permission or I have excellent reason to think that you would. (Thus, I'm allowed to organize your office as a surprise, but only if I am very certain that it is a surprise you would welcome. Otherwise, on Kant's view, it would be an unwarranted intrusion.) The duty of beneficence is a duty to promote the happiness of others as they understand it. I do not get to impose on other people my own ideas of what would make them happy.

Kant's account of beneficence is not universally shared. In particular, many philosophers have rejected the idea that we have so much latitude over how and when we fulfill our duties of beneficence. Certainly utilitarians reject this idea. As we saw in Chapter 2, utilitarians claim that our fundamental moral obligation is to bring about the greatest happiness for the greatest number of people, where happiness is understood as pleasure and the absence of pain. All of my actions must be directed toward maximizing happiness, not just for myself but for everyone. If it would maximize happiness (as it almost certainly would) for me to give up my afternoon Starbucks habit and send the money I save to Oxfam, then I am morally obligated to do so. It's true that I would experience a loss of pleasure and Starbucks a loss of revenue, but this would surely be outweighed by the misery of hunger or disease alleviated by my contribution. (The most well-known contemporary utilitarian, Peter Singer, has argued that we should be giving our resources to the poor to the point of marginal utility, or the point at which giving more would make us worse off than the people we are trying to help.[10])

The centrality of beneficence to utilitarianism has led people to focus on the major changes in our behavior that most utilitarians think are morally required of us. But utilitarianism has application to the more mundane questions of everyday giving and receiving. In the *Seinfeld* example with which I began this book, it's clear that the quest for wine and chocolate babka does not maximize happiness. (This is particularly the case because they can only come up with cinnamon babka, and they know that someone else is bringing the host chocolate babka.) It makes all four of them miserable and in true *Seinfeld* fashion, they spread their misery to the people around them. By utilitarian standards, they would have done much better to follow George's original suggestion about Pepsi and Ring Dings.

Still, utilitarianism has the implication that I should give a gift or do a favor whenever my doing so would maximize happiness. Gift-giving thus can become an absolute moral requirement. In theory, I could even be morally required to give a gift or do a favor that I know the other person doesn't want, so long as I am sure that it will maximize happiness. Now in practice, this is not very likely to happen. If I give someone an orange sweater when I know he hates the color, I am probably not going to be maximizing happiness. More likely, I will be wasting a lot of time shopping for something that is just going to sit at the back of the closet. But if I really am certain that my gift or favor will maximize happiness, utilitarianism gives me the green light whether or not it's what the recipient wants. (In theory, the fact that it makes me really happy to organize your office could outweigh your displeasure at my intrusion.)

On the other hand, utilitarianism might also require that I not give a gift on occasion where it might be expected, but where giving it would not maximize happiness. Let's suppose that I am invited to a very large wedding. I know that most of the other guests will be giving the couple elaborate gifts and that they live in a small apartment. Do they really need seventeen place settings of china? Or would I be better off taking that money and sending it to the local homeless shelter? Lots of people, particularly those with a heightened consciousness about the effects of consumerism on the environment and on people around the globe, think this is the best solution. And certainly there are many potential recipients who would rather get this kind of gift instead of yet another knick-knack.

Let's return to Amazon's new system of diverting unwanted gifts. On the surface, it looks like it will prove to be happiness-maximizing. The recipient is saved the trouble of returning something unwanted and he gets what he wants instead. The negative environmental impacts of returned gifts are avoided. And the giver is none the wiser for it. It might also even pass muster with the Kantian account of beneficence. After all, on Kant's view, benefactors are supposed to be giving what the recipients actually want. Gifts that are careless or unthinking are not, in Kant's eyes, especially good gifts. But supposing that the giver really is trying to please the recipient, we might think that she would be glad for a system that enables the recipient to exchange it for something he likes better. In that case, it wouldn't even be necessary to send Aunt Mildred a deceptive thank you for the original gift. If her goal is to give you something that you really want or need, then Amazon is helping her out.

And yet, there's still something missing from this analysis, conveniently simple as it is. Anna Post's objection to the system, recall, is that it turns gift-giving into something that too closely resembles other transactions, like simply shopping for oneself at a store (except with someone else's money). Gift cards, which are not widely loved among etiquette experts, can have this effect. The appeal of gift cards is that they occupy a kind of middle ground between a thoughtfully chosen present and plain old cash. A gift card to someone's favorite store shows that the giver has gone to the trouble of identifying the favorite store and acquiring a gift card, while still enabling the recipient to choose something that suits his own tastes. Gift cards are undeniably useful in many circumstances, particularly those where giving cash might feel a bit crass or inappropriate, but where the recipient's preferences are either hard to know or difficult to satisfy. For instance, a grandmother might really want to give teenage granddaughter a great new outfit, but might also know perfectly well that she has no clue what her granddaughter would consider stylish. Given the difficulty of finding a suitable gift herself, a gift card seems like a good compromise.

Even so, there is something about the routine exchange of gift cards that strikes many people as missing much of the point of giving gifts in the first place. Suppose I always give you a $50 gift card to Best Buy and you always give me a $50 gift card to Barnes and Noble. (Or perhaps we both just give each other $50 Amazon gift certificates.) Wouldn't it be easier if we each just went out and spent $50 on ourselves at our favorite store? Of course, then we're no longer doing a gift exchange at all. We're just shopping for ourselves. If Post is right that a genuine gift exchange is supposed to be something unlike other transactions, what is it that makes it different? And why would Amazon's gift-diversion system detract from it?

Amazon's technology is a new solution to an already existing problem—that of being on the receiving end of things that we do not want. This is more of a problem in our consumer-oriented society than it would have been in times past, or in places in the world with far less access to inexpensive consumer goods. It is a result of our material wealth that we can easily end up with so many things that we neither want nor need; a society in which everything is valuable is a society in which few gifts are useless or undesirable. But in twenty-first-century American culture, where the variety of things one can give or receive is seemingly endless, it is a very real problem, for both etiquette and ethics.

One solution to the over-consumption problem, of course, would be for us to radically change our gift-giving practices. Perhaps we should stop giving gifts altogether, or else mark occasions only with donations to worthy causes, used items, or consumable gifts like food. If the underlying moral goal of gift-giving is primarily to express some kind of appreciation or recognition for the recipient, there is no reason why the rules of etiquette can't change in accordance with an increased awareness of the harmful effects of overconsumption. Etiquette rules about smoking have, of course, changed dramatically over the last several decades in light of new information about the negative health effects of cigarettes on both the smoker and those around her. Perhaps etiquette rules concerning gift-giving will change as well. Such a change, like a change in the practice of smoking, would be driven by an improved understanding of our moral obligations to ourselves and others and what those obligations require of us. If my argument in Chapter 2 is correct, the rules of etiquette should follow wherever the moral principles that justify them lead.[11]

But until that happens, what do we do about gifts that we don't want or need? Etiquette experts generally agree that it is permissible to return, exchange, or give away unwanted gifts. In response to a question about what to do with an unwanted book given by a relative, Judith Martin says the following:

> Miss Manners does not realize why more people are not aware that presents and advice may easily be accepted without ever being used. Every tot knows instinctively that the way to accept unwanted mothering is to say, "Certainly, Mother," and then do nothing about it. Should your relative make the further mistake of asking if you have read the book or changed your life in accord with its dictates, the polite reply is, "Not yet, but I'm looking forward to it."[12]

Once the gift has been accepted and appropriate thanks given, the recipient is free to do with it what she likes, including selling it at a yard sale or regifting it to someone else. The only condition is that the recipient must take pains to hide the fate of the gift from the giver. During a *Seinfeld* episode about regifting (and degifting—still unsanctioned by etiquette), Tim Whatley fails to live up to this part of the recipient's obligation. He gives Jerry a label maker that Elaine gave him without attending to the likelihood that as Jerry's friend, Elaine would be likely to find out what he did with it.[13]

The giver, for her part, is supposed to turn a blind eye to what happens to the gift, not noticing, for instance, that it is never displayed or that despite being fragile, it is placed in the favorite play area of rambunctious children. The fact that a gift is unwanted or disliked may be known perfectly well to both parties, but politeness demands that they put on the pretense that this is not the case.

On the surface, Amazon's system doesn't look all that different from exchanging the sweater at a brick and mortar store. But perhaps it is. According to Martin, the important point is the *acceptance* of the gift or advice, not the use of it. One is not supposed to refuse a gift unless it was clearly intended as an insult or violates other norms.[14] Accepting the present seems to be part of the expression of gratitude; if I reject the present, it's hard to make the case that I am grateful for it. Perhaps justification for the Amazon system depends on whether its method is more like accepting, then disposing of the gift, or whether it is more like refusing the gift in the first place. If it's the latter, then the problem could be that the system gets in the way of gratitude. Insofar as accepting a gift is a valuable part of the exchange, then diverting a gift before it is ever received may undermine gratitude. In that case, it would be relevantly different from accepting a gift that one later exchanges or gives away.

Gift exchanges are, of course, about both giving and receiving. In fact, the cultural norms surrounding the reception of gifts are as complicated as those surrounding the giving of gifts.[15] If the value of the practice of gift-giving includes the receiving of the gift and the expression of gratitude, then a utilitarian analysis of that practice will take into account the entire exchange. Amazon's system might make gift-giving easier or more streamlined, but it might also contribute to an environment in which gift exchanges are generally less satisfying or meaningful to the participants, and in which gratitude loses its importance. If so, then although Amazon's system might maximize happiness in isolated instances, its widespread use might not be happiness-maximizing after all. Maybe a world in which everyone exchanges only Visa gift cards is a world in which we've lost everything that makes gift-giving valuable in the first place. In that case, utilitarianism might recommend that we put up with the occasional hideous sweater from Aunt Mildred as a small sacrifice in the service of something very important.

I have suggested that Amazon's technology might interfere with gratitude. Let us now turn to the question of what makes gratitude so important and so complicated in the first place. Kant, as I have said, considered it to be a duty of love, and many people think of it as a virtue. Gratitude is partly an attitude, but an attitude that needs to issue in concrete actions if it is to attain its moral point. Ideally, I would both feel grateful for what I am given and express that gratitude appropriately. If I am not in fact feeling grateful, politeness normally directs me to express the gratitude anyway.

It's unclear whether gratitude should be pegged to the intention or effort of the giver, or to the actual benefit conferred by the gift or favor. Probably, it is both. If someone with the best of intentions tries to do me a favor, but ends up making me worse off, I should be grateful for her efforts, but it's not necessarily inappropriate for me to express it in less effusive terms than I would have done had she been successful in those efforts. Thus, if someone tries to help me by ridding my computer of a virus, but ends up erasing my hard drive in the process, I am likely to feel less grateful than if she had done it successfully. Moreover, it seems that I am justified in expressing more gratitude in the latter case, given that the benefit to me was much greater.

Likewise, if someone with a magical talent for restoring hard drives manages to get mine back with a few keystrokes, it is appropriate for me to fall all over myself thanking her, despite the fact that she expended comparatively little effort.

In order for gratitude to be morally appropriate at all, however, the giver has to be aiming at the recipient's good. We can see this when we consider gifts that come with strings attached, such as when Tim, the label maker regifter, gives Elaine a Superbowl ticket expecting that she will sleep with him in return. Obviously such gifts can be refused without violating the demands of etiquette. They also do not require gratitude, since the intent is not to benefit the recipient. (Indeed, we may not even want to call these gifts at all.) The same might be said about gifts that are actually disguised insults, such as a weight loss book or a fur coat given to a known animal rights advocate. If we know that the giver's intention is to embarrass or humiliate us, it's hard to make the case that we even need to say "Thank you," much less feel grateful. Likewise, a favor or bit of advice that is excessively intrusive or overbearing can be flatly declined without incurring a charge of ingratitude.

Kant was especially sensitive to the potentially destabilizing effects that beneficence can have on a relationship. In Chapter 4, I discussed the importance he placed on maintaining moral equality with other people. When it comes to beneficence, he suggests that benefactors must make an effort to ensure that the benefit doesn't undermine the recipient's self-respect:

> He must also carefully avoid any appearance of intending to bind the other by it; for if he showed that he wanted to put the other under an obligation (which always humbles the other in his own eyes), it would be not a true benefit that he rendered him. Instead he must show that he is himself put under obligation by the other's acceptance or honored by it, hence that the duty is merely something that

he owes, unless (as is better) he can practice his beneficence in complete secrecy.[16]

Kant clearly thinks that it is better to give than receive, that to be a recipient of someone else's generosity, while pleasant in some respects, has dangers of its own. The feeling of being in someone's debt, Kant thought, is one that self-respecting people want to avoid having, and that truly considerate people want to avoid creating. Hence, he suggests that when we give gifts or do favors, we do our best to give the impression that we are discharging a debt of our own when we are giving the gift or doing the favor. Or better, we should do such things in secret.

Of course, when gifts are given in secret, they lose at least some of their expressive force. A recipient of an anonymous gift may know that he is respected or admired, but not by whom. This adds to the mystery, but it means that the gift does not communicate the respect or admiration of a particular giver. It also makes it rather difficult for the recipient to reciprocate down the line. Anonymous favors pose the same problem, which is perhaps why people feel compelled to track down Good Samaritans so that they can at least express their gratitude. And anonymous advice is potentially the most dangerous of all, since it raises the likelihood that it will be expressed unkindly.

For the most part, the practice of exchanging things like gifts and favors works best when it is reciprocal. One-sidedness can make givers feel as though they are being taken advantage of, and it can also make recipients feel demeaned or dependent. On the Kantian view, the mutuality of the exchange is important because it enables both parties to maintain their own self-respect and continue to respect the other person as a moral equal. Certainly, some relationships are inevitably more one-sided than others, such as the relationship between parents and children. And there may be periods of time in which a morally healthy relationship involves lopsided giving and receiving, such as when one person in the relationship is suffering from a serious illness. In such cases, heartfelt gratitude may be the only repayment possible or necessary.

It is not exactly a startling revelation to say that the practice of giving and receiving gifts, favors, and advice is fraught with complexity. Everyone knows this from experience, and we see it reflected in the extensive discussions of these matters in etiquette books and columns. In this chapter, I have suggested that these etiquette problems have a common moral basis in the duty of beneficence. Philosophical accounts of beneficence vary considerably, and it is unlikely that, for instance, a utilitarian would come up with the same rules about gift-giving that a Kantian would. Whether using Amazon's new system would be rude depends on how one thinks about gift-giving and its purpose.

The conventions of giving and receiving things matter less than the moral attitudes they convey. In a culture in which people routinely give each other cash, it may well be interpreted as a very considerate gift, not at all crass or unthinking. Unsolicited advice may be seen as kindly, not disrespectful, particularly if it is reciprocal. It is possible that American culture is evolving in such a way that using technology to divert unwanted gifts will soon seem normal and inoffensive, at least to most people. Meanwhile, we might do well to follow Judith Martin's suggestions for gift-giving: "A more positive approach is to select something among those things of which one cannot ever have enough . . . What falls into this category? Bottles of wine, diamonds, and homemade cookies."[17]

Neighbors
Seven

> I'd rather have the thieves than the neighbors—the thieves don't
> impose . . . The neighbors want your time. The thieves want your
> things. I'd rather give them things than time.[1]
>
> Larry David

Larry David is likely not the world's best example of a good
neighbor, but his frustration with the demands of neighborliness
is one that most of us have probably experienced at some point
or other. Much of the action in *Curb Your Enthusiasm* and its
predecessor *Seinfeld* involves interactions between the main
characters and their neighbors. Because everyone has neighbors,
it is easy to identify with the kinds of problems raised on the
shows. Indeed, relationships with neighbors, both good and bad,
have been a staple of literature and television for quite some time.
Even Jane Austen comments on the difficulties of neighbor
relationships. In *Pride and Prejudice*, Mr. Bennet remarks, "For what
do we live, but to make sport for our neighbours, and laugh at
them in our turn?"[2] Mr. Bennet is being his usual sarcastic self
when he makes this remark, but it nevertheless reflects a truth of
which we are all very well aware, which is that our relationships
with our neighbors, whether friendly or not, play an enormously
important role in our day-to-day lives.

The fact that we live in close physical proximity to our
neighbors generates a host of etiquette issues, many of which are
covered in etiquette books and columns. In this chapter, I will

argue that this physical proximity also raises moral issues that make neighbor relationships substantively different from other relationships with strangers or acquaintances.

Mr. Bennet is reacting to the gossip about the Bennet family being reported in a letter from his cousin, the intrusive Mr. Collins. Mr. Bennet, unlike Elizabeth, is amused by the reports circulating about Lydia and Elizabeth, and not terribly concerned with the fact that their private family affairs are a topic of discussion among their neighbors. He takes it for granted that neighbors will gossip about each other, and that it is more or less a reciprocal form of amusement. They derive enjoyment from getting a close look at our lives and we in turn derive enjoyment from getting a close look at theirs.

Sometimes, of course, our neighbors are also our friends, as in the long-running sitcom *Friends*. On that show, it is the fact that the characters are friends that matters most; the fact that they live in neighboring apartments is not normally very important to what happens on the show. But in many, if not most cases, our neighbors are not also our friends, at least not in the traditional sense of being friends. This means that neighbor relationships are not quite like other relationships that we have. We choose our friends and can also choose to stop being someone's friend, but except in unusual circumstances, we cannot choose our neighbors. We simply find ourselves with them, for better or for worse.

The nineteenth-century German philosopher Arthur Schopenhauer penned a fable in which he described the plight of porcupines attempting to huddle together on a cold day.[3] The desire for warmth draws them closer together, but once they succeed in getting close, they begin to prick each other with their quills. Eventually, after some trial and error, they discover the distance at which they are close enough to benefit from their shared body heat, but not so close that their quills pose a danger. The plight of the porcupines, of course, is supposed to represent the plight of human beings who find ourselves driven together in order to fulfill certain needs and yet repelled by the kinds of constraints, demands, and annoyances that living with other people brings. Schopenhauer's fable of the porcupines is a somewhat darker, more pessimistic version of Kant's story about love and respect. We are drawn to other people, whether by love or by necessity, while at the same time pulling back from them, whether for reasons of respect or because we are pricked by their quills. Living well with one's neighbors is a matter of finding the right place between excessive closeness and excessive distance.

Like Mr. Bennet, we all know just how difficult it is to keep one's affairs entirely hidden from one's neighbors, particular if the neighbors are right on the other side of a wall or floorboard. Regardless of our wishes, we are participants in the lives of our neighbors. We know the hours they keep, the kinds of visitors they receive, and their preferred methods for disciplining their children. We are privy to their arguments and their parties, just by virtue of the fact that it is often impossible for us not to hear them. We are also sometimes called upon to help them in medical and household emergencies. Indeed, their emergencies can become our emergencies, a fact to which anyone who has lived below someone with an overflowing bathtub can attest.

In older etiquette books, discussions about neighbors mostly focus on the complexities of visiting or paying calls. The practice of calling on people was, of course, a primary form of social life until quite recently, and was heavily structured by rules of etiquette. These rules dictated when calls should be paid, by whom, to whom, and for how long, as well as what should be said and served. Failing with respect to one's obligations of calling would have been a serious breach of etiquette and an obvious show of disrespect, as *Pride and Prejudice*'s Jane Bennet finds out the hard way when Caroline Bingley pays only a short, long overdue call.

The practice of paying formal calls has long since died out, although some semblances of it remain. Our social horizons are now much broader, and we no longer depend on our neighbors to provide us with the bulk of our social life. Contemporary etiquette books reflect this shift, spending little or no time on the subject of paying calls and much more on the subject of simply getting along with one's neighbors. Judith Martin devotes most of a chapter to neighbor etiquette in *Miss Manners' Guide to Domestic Tranquility*. In it, she answers questions about dealing with overly friendly neighbors as well as overly aloof ones, neighbors who are offended by one's artwork, neighbors who honk their horns excessively, and neighbors who do not close their shades when they should. Likewise, the 16th edition of Emily Post's *Etiquette*, rewritten by Peggy Post, contains a section called "Good Neighborliness" in which she covers, among other things, noise problems, parking problems, pets, and backyard swimming pools.

It's obvious enough that living near people raises etiquette problems. It's less obvious how it raises moral problems, at least on a day-to-day basis. Many people do consider neighborliness to be a virtue. It was not on Aristotle's list of virtues, although friendliness was. To be virtuously friendly, on Aristotle's view, is to occupy a middle ground between being ingratiating and being surly or cantankerous. It is a kind of pleasant, cheerful demeanor in greeting and conversing with people. I assume that neighborliness requires friendliness, at least most of the time. But there is more to neighborliness as a virtue than giving someone a friendly wave as you get your mail.

Within moral philosophy, it has long been recognized that proximity plays an important role in our obligations of beneficence. The fact that I happen to be near someone who needs help means that I am under more of a moral obligation to help that person than I would be if I were further away. This is partly a matter of practicality—the nearer someone is, the more quickly they can administer CPR or jump a car with a dead battery. But it's not just about practicality. Many of us feel a special responsibility to people in our neighborhoods and communities—a kind of common bond that makes us into each other's keepers.

Less obvious (and less well discussed in philosophy) are the ways in which proximity affects our duties of respect. Being in close proximity to someone makes it both more necessary and more challenging to communicate appropriate respect to that person. In this chapter, I will again draw on the work of Erving Goffman to discuss how our social behavior can be used to convey moral attitudes like respect and serve moral purposes like maintaining appropriate distance.

I will begin with a discussion of how proximity affects our relationship with people with whom we are temporarily neighbors, such as when we are in elevators or airplane rows and find ourselves sitting or standing very close to other people. This will enable us to see how moral principles about respect, consideration, and helpfulness shape the specific etiquette rules and norms that govern our behavior in tight quarters. I will then extend this analysis to a discussion of more permanent neighbors, people with whom we expect to be in close proximity for months or years. Neighbor relationships, I will suggest, operate under different moral norms than other kinds of relationships. In turn, those moral norms shape the etiquette rules that most effectively govern interactions with neighbors.

We often find that people are more insistent about following and enforcing the rules of etiquette in circumstances where they are likely to find themselves sharing small spaces with strangers. This includes elevators, buses, subway cars, airplanes, waiting rooms, and crowded city sidewalks. Behavior in such circumstances is governed by unwritten, but widely followed rules. Consider, for instance, the conventions for riding elevators in the United States: face the doors, keep eye contact to a minimum, lower your voice, stop highly personal conversations, make only brief remarks to strangers about neutral topics like the rainy weather or the slow speed of the elevator, and so forth.

Failure to follow the rules draws disapproval, sometimes expressed and sometimes not. The rider who faces the back of the elevator when there is room for him to turn around, or makes prolonged eye contact with other riders will be regarded as eccentric and possibly even dangerous. His fellow riders may very well shrink back against the elevator walls and breathe a sigh of relief when he gets off. Likewise, people who carry on conversations too loudly or discuss overly personal topics will generate uncomfortable reactions among fellow riders, who may find themselves having to work extra hard to pretend not to be listening.

Why should elevators bring out this peculiarly rigid form of behavior? In Chapter 3, I mentioned that Americans tend to maintain more physical distance from other people than do members of other cultures. Elevators and other tight spaces make it nearly impossible to maintain that physical distance when they become crowded. We are forced to stand or sit closer to strangers than we ordinarily feel comfortable doing. The result is a form of unsought intimacy. Because our social practices generally direct us to avoid overt familiarity with strangers, we find ourselves with a rather pressing problem of both etiquette and ethics. How can we communicate the ordinary respect that we owe strangers when we are so close that we may even be touching each other?

One of the most effective ways to offset the discomfort of close physical proximity with strangers is to create other forms of distance. In a crowded elevator, we manage this by way of our behavior and body language. By standing stiffly with our arms and bags close to our body, we reduce the likelihood that we will make physical contact with our fellow passengers. Staring up at the elevator numbers has practical value, but it is also a way of ensuring as little eye contact as possible. Because anyone on an elevator can hear what anyone else is saying, it is impossible to avoid eavesdropping. Lowering one's voice and not talking about private matters is a way of preventing others from feeling as though they are part of a conversation that social norms say they should not overhear.

All these practices, which most of us do without thinking about it and which are well-documented by researchers, can be understood as ways of expressing respect to our fellow travelers. But there is another aspect to the proximity issue. Riding on an elevator with other people also generates certain responsibilities toward them, some of which can feel like minor moral obligations. The person who is nearest to the buttons is obliged to select floors for other passengers on polite request; refusal is nearly always rude. Generally speaking, it is incumbent on elevator passengers to hold open the door for people who are standing right outside or who clearly need more time to get on the elevator than the standard elevator door settings allow, such as people riding in wheelchairs or pushing strollers. Of course there may be disagreements about how long to hold a door for a rider still several yards away from the door, or the extent to which passengers must crowd together in order to accommodate additional riders. There may also be conventions quite specific to a given elevator setting. (Thus, when the elevator is one of several, there is less obligation to hold the door, but when it is a single elevator known to be slow, that obligation increases.) But there are always conventions at work.

When we step back and consider them, we can see that the etiquette norms of riding elevators traverse a fine line between acknowledging and ignoring the presence of other people. We cannot simply pretend that they aren't there, that we are on the elevator by ourselves. We have to respond to their reasonable requests and be conscious of how our body language is being interpreted. And yet, respect for them demands that we engage in the most minimal physical and social contact possible so as to limit the negative experience and effects of the unchosen intimacy.

Goffman describes a way of interacting with people that he calls "civil inattention." It is something that we do without thinking, but it plays a very important role in the way we interact with strangers:

> What seems to be involved is that one gives to another enough visual notice to demonstrate that one appreciates that the other is present (and that one admits openly to having seen him), while at the next moment withdrawing one's attention from him so as to express that he does not constitute a target of special curiosity or design.[4]

Goffman goes on to describe in detail how this affects our behavior on the street, claiming that we eye people until we are about eight feet away from them, at which point we cast our eyes down as we walk past.[5] Civil inattention, he thinks, is a constant feature of our interactions with strangers, and the closer the proximity, the more important it becomes:

> The closer the onlookers are to the individual who interests them, the more exposed his position (and theirs), and the more obligation they will feel to ensure him civil inattention. The further they are from him, the more license they will feel to stare at him a little.[6]

Civil inattention becomes a way for us to acknowledge other people's presence and, I would add, their standing to make claims on our help, without drawing so close that we treat them disrespectfully. The initial eye contact indicates that I regard the other person as an end in Kant's sense and that I am prepared to act in ways that reflect this, such as by pressing the "door open" button for him. Eye contact, as Goffman says, "opens one up for face engagement."[7]

Goffman claims that we can be obligated to keep ourselves open for face engagement. He does not say why, but we can fill in the argument by returning to Kant. We might say that face engagement is important to expressing acknowledgement of the other person's moral status. By making myself open to the other person's contact, I treat her as an end in Kant's sense, as someone who can legitimately call upon my help if needed. Likewise, the subsequent aversion of my eyes communicates my recognition that respecting the other person also means granting her a certain degree of privacy and personal space. We know that staring at someone is rude, but Goffman's analysis enables us to say why. If I stare at a stranger, I treat her as an object of curiosity or visual pleasure (or displeasure). Treating her this way may express the attitude that her only purpose is to satisfy my desire for visual interest, in which case I am failing to treat her as a Kantian end. Averting my eyes is a way of respecting her moral status and acknowledging that she is not simply a decorative or bizarre object. (This, of course, also explains the etiquette rule that it is rude to stare at someone with an unusual physical feature or disability.) The closer I am standing to the person, the more important the aversion of eye contact becomes as an expression of my respect.

People who do not follow the rules in elevators without meeting any obvious excusing conditions are, as I mentioned above, normally regarded with suspicion.[8] In Goffman's picture, this is largely because the person thereby shows himself to be unpredictable, someone who is not concerned to do his part to shore up and sustain the social order. From a moral standpoint, the person who refuses to abide by the standard elevator rules expresses a lack of respect for the other person. Refusing to make initial eye contact is a failure to acknowledge the person's standing at all; making prolonged eye contact communicates that the other person can be treated as an object for visual inspection. Standing too close communicates excessive intimacy, unbounded by respect for privacy.

The problems that we face about intimacy in elevators are, if we are lucky, very short-lived. But when we live next door to people, or above or below them, unsought intimacy is part of our everyday lives. The problem is not normally one of familiarity created by physical contact; rather, it is produced by the intimate knowledge that we have of our neighbors' lives, along with our special responsibilities to help them when they are in need of it. Martin puts it this way:

> Urban neighborliness means that one has an obligation to notice disreputable characters who seem to be fooling around with a neighbor's house, and to report them. Urban neighborliness also means that one has an obligation not to notice disreputable characters whom one's neighbor has invited to his house for purposes of fooling around.[9]

Martin is undoubtedly right about the requirement of neighborliness, but it is obvious how difficult this is to put into practice. One must be observant, but not too observant. Or if one has accidentally been too observant, it is necessary to pretend that one has not. Indeed, the pretense discussed in Chapter 4 becomes especially important when we are talking about people who live near each other.

Civil inattention is just as important in apartment buildings or closely spaced housing developments as it is in elevators, although it takes a different form. In his writings, Goffman discusses what he calls the "nod" line, which is the point at which members of a community are expected to acknowledge each other, and according to Goffman, it is determined by the size of the community.

> In Anglo-American society there exists a kind of "nod line" that can be drawn at a particular point through a rank order of communities according to size. Any community below

the line, and hence below a certain size, will subject its adults, whether acquainted or not, to mutual greetings; any community above the line will free all pairs of unacquainted persons from this obligation. (Where the line is drawn varies, of course, according to region.) In the case of communities that fall above the nod line, even persons who cognitively recognize each other to be neighbors, and know that this state of mutual information exists, may sometimes be careful to refrain from engaging each other. Perhaps this is done on the theory that, once acquaintance-ship is established between persons living near one another, it might become difficult to keep sufficient distance in the relationship.[10]

The existence of the nod line is well known to anyone who has spent time in both a small American town and a large city. No one walking down a sidewalk in a major city nods to strangers on a routine basis. It is both impractical, given the sheer number of people on the sidewalk, and subject to misinterpretation. Nor do urban conventions ordinarily demand that one do anything more than nod to a neighbor or other acquaintance. One may, according to Martin, even pretend that one does not see them. As she puts it, "urban life requires a balance of sociability with privacy. For this reason, certain conventions are necessary, enabling people to ignore one another at times without being rude."[11]

The right to be ignored on occasion and the associated duty to ignore our neighbors on occasion is paramount to good relations between neighbors. Indeed, we might go so far as to say that it is not just acceptable, but morally necessary to pretend that one does not see one's neighbors in certain contexts where they might reasonably not want to be seen, such as when they are fetching the newspaper in especially ratty old pajamas. To put it in Goffman's terms, it is yet another way in which we help people maintain the fronts that are essential to their self-respect or to their happiness.

How does occasionally ignoring our neighbors contribute to their well-being? One explanation is that it makes possible a greater degree of privacy. Emily Post, who valued privacy quite highly herself, put it this way:

> One of the greatest advantages that money grants is the boon of privacy to those who can live in a house guarded by servants, who can build high walls around their garden, who can devise a retreat of her own where they can work or dream or spend the previous hours as they choose. But this protected tranquility is within the reach of the very few. In millions of homes, safety from interruption is granted only by the consideration of friends and neighbors.[12]

Having spent much of her life in New York City, Post was sensitive to the complexities of crowded urban life, although her wealth would certainly have insulated her from the worst of it. Privacy is of course more of an issue in apartments and condominiums than in single-family houses, but it is important anywhere that people live in sight and hearing distance of one another. Although Post herself didn't explicitly endorse the practice of occasionally pretending that we don't see our neighbors, it is undoubtedly one way to achieve the kind of privacy and tranquility that she thinks is so necessary. If our neighbors are occasionally willing to pretend that they don't see us, we can sometimes pretend that we are alone when we are not. This is certainly restful, but there is something more to it than that.

In Chapter 4, I employed Goffman's distinction between front regions and back regions in defending the need for mutual cooperation in sustaining a polite front region. When it comes to neighbors with whom we are not also friends, our natural tendency is to keep the relationship in that front region. But our physical proximity means that the back region has a tendency to intrude. Pretending not to see people getting the newspaper in their pajamas is a way of keeping that back region at bay. For most people, pajamas are backstage clothing, not something in which we want to be seen on the streets. When my neighbor pretends not to notice my pajamas, she helps me sustain the front that I do not appear in public unless I am properly dressed.[13]

Sometimes the intrusion of the back region cannot so easily be ignored. Consider, for instance, the experience of sitting next to someone in a crowded airplane row. In such circumstances, it is very difficult to avoid physical contact with one's neighbor's legs and arms, something that is ordinarily back region behavior among people we know well. Airplane seating creates normally unwelcome intimacy with strangers because it forces the back region to intrude into what are ideally front region interactions. We accept, of course, that some intimacy is inevitable for the duration of the flight, but the expectation is that it will be minimized and ended as soon as possible.

Our physical proximity to our neighbors also means that we must be prepared to be called upon and to offer help in a variety of ways, help that we are more obliged to offer in virtue of being on the scene. If my seatmate in row 17 spills his coffee, I am obligated to help him clean it up in a way that someone seated in row 32 is not. The same is true for people we live near. Sometimes the help we offer neighbors will be an ordinary, non-intimate form, such as shoveling snow when a neighbor is recovering from surgery. But sometimes the assistance takes on a more personal form. If my neighbor has a medical emergency in the middle of the night, or needs help getting rid of a bat or squirrel in his house, I may find myself in his bedroom, closet, bathroom—spaces that we normally try to keep in the back region. This can create a great deal of awkwardness, some of which can be defused with humor or similar skills. But then after the crisis is over, we are obliged to return our relationship to the front region. It would be impolite for me to make a remark a week later about the weirdly large number of shampoo bottles I saw in his bathroom. To do so is an unwelcome reminder of the one-sided intimacy that his need for my help created. Returning our relationship to the front region is important because it preserves his self-respect and enables us to meet once again as moral equals.

The fact that we can so readily find ourselves in the middle of our neighbor's most intimate events and experiences means that keeping a respectful distance is both more important and more difficult. I may know all the details of my neighbors' violent argument last night, but I still need to engage in ordinary interactions with them the next day at the bus stop or in the elevator. Of course, not all intrusions of the back region can be ignored or forgotten. If I hear my neighbor abusing her young children through our shared apartment wall, I have to do something about it. My calling Child Protective Services on her will obviously make it impossible for us to maintain the usual polite neighborly relationships, but this is a case where the moral obligation to protect her children from harm overrides the obligation to maintain a respectful distance by pretending I do not hear what she is doing.

I began this chapter by suggesting that physical proximity to other people, whether temporary or permanent, affects the nature of our moral relationship to them, both in terms of beneficence and respect. Our obligations of beneficence are often greater by virtue of our proximity, but the fact that they may land us into unexpectedly intimate situations means that respect is especially important. Mutual pretense is an important part of being able to maintain both sanity and privacy when living near others. The back region inevitably intrudes, but part of being a good neighbor means ignoring back region behavior and circumstances when possible and minimizing them when not. Of course, the intimacy created by a neighbor relationship can be an enormous benefit to our lives. Neighbors do sometimes become friends. But even when they do not, the virtue of neighborliness, and its associated skills of civil inattention and tactful pretense, is something worth cultivating.

Eight

For nearly a thousand years, the same ghastly fear has been gripping humanity. Death? Disease? Starvation? Annihilation? No, forks.[1]

Judith Martin

By now, it should be evident that I do not think that etiquette is mostly, or even primarily, about which fork to use. On the other hand, it would be hard to deny that actual etiquette books, both past and present, devote a great deal of space to matters like setting the table for a formal dinner, issuing invitations correctly, choosing appropriate attire for social occasions, and so forth. Casual readers can be excused for thinking that such matters are a primary concern of etiquette, if not the primary concern. Moreover, rules about forks and invitation wording are also the kinds of etiquette rules that seem least congenial to my analysis of etiquette conventions as vehicles for communicating moral aims like respect and consideration. It is not easy to see how a correct table setting could possibly convey anything morally significant.

By itself, of course, it does not. The placement or misplacement of a wine glass is entirely trivial from the standpoint of morality. But what is not trivial is the larger practice in which the rule about placing wine glasses has its place. That larger practice is what, in contemporary life, is usually called "entertaining." For reasons I will explain shortly, I am going call it the practice of hospitality instead. And hospitality *is* a practice with moral significance. Indeed, the virtue of hospitality has a long and venerable tradition. In this chapter, the rather challenging aim will be to show the connection between the practice of hospitality and etiquette rules about matters like forks and wine glasses. I will make that connection by exploring the moral implications of good taste. But first, let me say something more about hospitality itself.

In recent years, the idea of hospitality as a virtue has fallen somewhat by the wayside. Many of us now associate the word with the hotel and restaurant business, the members of which refer to their work as the hospitality industry. The practice of offering hospitality to people in one's home is, as I noted above, now normally called "entertaining."[2] Most of what I will be talking about in this chapter falls into the category of entertaining. But I will not call it that because the word makes the practice sound superficial, as if it were mostly about cooking and decorating. It's not that cooking and decorating are themselves superficial; quite the contrary, they are part of something that is deeply important to human flourishing. But it's easier to show what is so important about these things if we talk about them in terms of hospitality.

Hospitality as a virtue has a long history. In the Christian tradition, it dates back at least 1,500 years to St. Benedict of Nursia, whose widely followed rules for monastic life include specific instructions about receiving visitors. The Rule of St. Benedict directs that anyone who comes to the door, wealthy or poor, should be welcomed as Jesus. This rule and the tradition of Christian hospitality drawn from it (which has parallels in other religions) suggest that the practice of hospitality should be oriented toward the welfare, comfort, and dignity of the guest. To be a guest in someone's home is to hold a high status, warranting honor and special consideration. The obligations of the host are drawn from this understanding of the guest and what is necessary in order to welcome her presence and make her feel at home.

It is this sense of hospitality as the virtue of promoting the welfare and happiness of guests that I think gets somewhat lost when we talk in terms of entertaining instead. In this chapter, I will return to what we might call the traditional meaning of hospitality in exploring the relationship between hosts and guests. This relationship remains deeply morally significant for us, even as we've replaced St. Benedict with Martha Stewart. To be a good host, I will argue, demands both moral and practical skill that goes well beyond following a recipe and tracking down coordinating throw pillows for the living room.

Hospitality is an unusual virtue because unlike other virtues, it requires some skill in the realm of aesthetics. The virtue of hospitality, I will suggest, is in part a virtue of having good taste. This may be a controversial claim, since we are not accustomed to thinking of good taste as having any connection to virtue. It's hard to see how a person's moral character is implicated in her ability to assess the merits of a Merlot or find just the right wall sconce for that dark corner of the hallway. The very idea that there could be a close connection between good taste and good moral character may strike us as implausible on its face.

Indeed, the fact that contemporary America's icon of good taste, Martha Stewart, served time in prison for obstruction of justice and lying to investigators might seem to be definitive proof against it. Obviously it's possible to have wonderful taste, but questionable moral judgment. And likewise, there are people with sterling moral qualities who cannot match their pants to their shirts, much less create lovely Thanksgiving centerpieces out of items collected in the backyard before breakfast. All of this is true, of course. And yet by itself it doesn't undermine the idea that there might be a connection between good taste and good moral character. Let us explore this connection by thinking about what it means to have good taste in the first place.

David Hume argued that we are naturally inclined to be pleased and displeased by certain qualities, not just in other people, but in our surroundings. We approve, he argues, of what is useful; indeed, if we are properly disposed, we will think that what is useful is also beautiful:

> A ship appears more beautiful to an artist, or one moderately skilled in navigation, where its prow is wide and swelling beyond its poop, than if it were framed with a precise geometrical regularity, in contradiction to all the laws of mechanics. A building, whose doors and windows were exact squares, would hurt the eye by that very proportion; as ill adapted to the figure of a human creature, for whose service the fabric was intended.[3]

Hume thinks there is more to aesthetic appeal than utility, but he does believe that we take greater pleasure in inanimate objects that are designed in a way to be useful to us. In Hume's eyes, it would make sense that we would find a comfortable-looking sofa more appealing than one covered in scratchy fabric.

Emily Post, whose father was a well-known architect and who herself was quite well-informed about aesthetics, wrote extensively about good taste in both behavior and in home furnishings. In her 1948 book, *The Personality of a House: The Blue Book of Home Charm*, she takes a largely Humean approach to the question of what makes a home aesthetically pleasing. She remarks that "beauty that is worthy of the name must delight the eye, exalt the spirit, and satisfy the intelligence. But, first of all, there must be suitability to purpose and to situation."[4] Anticipating today's complaints about McMansions, she laments the practice of putting an excessively large house on a small lot or a Spanish-inspired patio in a cold climate where, as she says, "it serves principally as a container for half-frozen rain and snow."[5] Post, who for decades served as the American standard-bearer for good taste, based those standards firmly in the idea that a house's beauty derives from its ability to provide comfort, convenience, and warmth to those who live in it and visit it.

According to Post, there are four "essential requirements" of a house that must be fulfilled for the house to be considered tasteful:

> Every house must respond to four requirements: First, its outer appearance—its attractiveness, its neatness, as seen by the public passing by. Second, the first view of the interior —the general effect of the entrance hall or living and drawing-room of formal hospitality. Third, its intimate rooms satisfying to the needs of those who live in them. Fourth, its practical response to modern requirements of comfort.[6]

On her view, an expensively impeccably decorated house that bears no traces of its owner's personality may be beautiful, but it can never be tasteful. Neither can a kitchen in which it is impossible to cook efficiently. It is not money that makes for good taste in a house, but the ability to create a space that serves the intended purpose of that space.

These requirements suggest in order to make one's house tasteful, one must be able to see it through the eyes of other people, whether passers-by or members of the family. That is, for Post, the only way to tell whether the setting is attending to their needs and desires. For instance, she argues that children need space where they can play unhindered and make messes without destroying anything important. A house with children but with no such space will thereby fail to meet the third requirement, as would a house with nothing but oddly shaped chairs and poorly placed lamps.

Making other people feel comfortable in our houses is thus not simply a matter of the things that we do; it is also about the environment we create. Suppose that I have large, friendly dogs that shed profusely and have a tendency to drool on visitors in the excitement of greeting them. People who own such dogs do not generally mind dog hair and trails of saliva on their clothes, perhaps thinking that it's a small price to pay for the charm of a dog's company. But of course, not everyone is a dog lover, and even dog lovers sometimes show up to parties in outfits that require dry cleaning. A good dog-owning host needs to be able to take up the perspective of her guests in order to understand how the setting in which they find themselves affects their comfort. If I don't appreciate how intimidating my dogs might seem to a small child or how annoying dog drool can be to someone who takes meticulous care of his clothes, then I am failing to be hospitable. My ability to make my guests feel at ease depends on my skill at imagining what they will feel and experience upon entering my house.

We have discussed in previous chapters the moral importance of this skill at taking up the perspective of another person. Being able to imagine the scene through someone else's eyes enables us to attend to nuances of situation and setting that we would otherwise miss. Perhaps I genuinely don't notice dog hair on my own clothes, but if I can imagine being someone who does notice it, I will be able to reason better about how being covered in dog hair will affect her. I am able to see what would and would not make her comfortable, despite it being different from what I would need to ensure my own comfort. In this sense, hospitality requires a kind of imaginative, empathetic capacity.

In Chapter 3, I argued that the capacity for moral imagination and an appreciation for nuance is part of the virtue of practical wisdom. Aristotle described practical wisdom as a kind of perceptual capacity. The practically wise person can "see" what actions and behaviors fit well into the situation she faces. This perceptual capacity is part of what I have in mind when I say that good taste is required for the exercise of hospitality in a virtuous way. It is not simply about being able to put together colors in an interesting way; it's about being able to create a setting that will please one's guests and make them feel welcome. This is the essence of good taste and hence, successful hospitality.

The idea that there is a link between good taste and virtuous hospitality is nicely illustrated by Jane Austen in her portrayal of her most famous hero, *Pride and Prejudice*'s Fitzwilliam Darcy. In the novel, Elizabeth's visit to Pemberley, Darcy's estate, proves to be a turning point in their relationship. Darcy is extremely wealthy, and Pemberley is one of the grandest properties in any of Austen's novels. But it is not the grandeur that impresses Elizabeth so much as the unusually good taste that Pemberley reflects:

> It was a large, handsome stone building, standing well on rising ground, and backed by a ridge of high woody hills; and in front, a stream of some natural importance was swelled into greater, but without any artificial appearance. Its banks were neither formal nor falsely adorned. Elizabeth was delighted. She had never seen a place for which nature had done more, or where natural beauty had been so little counteracted by an awkward taste. They were all of them warm in their admiration; and at that moment, she felt that to be mistress of Pemberley might be something![7]

Later, when Elizabeth tells her sister Jane that she is engaged to Darcy, Jane asks her how long she has loved him. Elizabeth responds, "It has been coming on so gradually, that I hardly know when it began. But I believe I must date it from my first seeing his beautiful grounds at Pemberley."[8] Jane interprets the remark as being in jest, presumably because it purports to imply that Elizabeth's feelings for Darcy changed once she got a good look at his fabulous house. But although Elizabeth does undoubtedly mean the remark to be partly a joke, it is also partly true. The visit to Pemberley revealed aspects of Darcy's moral character that Elizabeth had not yet seen and, arguably, could not have seen except by visiting Darcy at his home.

Elizabeth first tours the estate not with Darcy, but with his housekeeper, who has nothing but praise for his character. Austen describes the rooms of Pemberley as "lofty and handsome" with "furniture suitable to the fortune of their proprietor."[9] But she qualifies this by noting that "Elizabeth saw, with admiration of his taste, that it was neither gaudy nor uselessly fine; with less of splendor, and more real elegance, than the furniture of Rosings."[10] Rosings Park, the home of the arrogant Lady Catherine de Bourgh, is also a very grand estate, but its décor is aimed at showing off the wealth, status, and power of its owner. Its goal (and usual effect) is to make visitors feel awestruck and humble.

Pemberley, by contrast, is far more welcoming. Darcy, unlike Lady Catherine, is not interested in displaying his wealth for visitors; rather, he is interested in using it to promote their happiness. Upon hearing that Elizabeth's uncle, Mr. Gardiner, enjoys fishing, Darcy immediately offers to equip him with fishing gear and invites him to take advantage of his stocked lake. Lady Catherine has a fine piano that no one in the house knows how to play; Darcy, by contrast, purchases one for the sole purpose of delighting his music-loving younger sister. Darcy at Pemberley turns out to be an excellent host, and his behavior there shows Elizabeth that he is not the ill-mannered snob that she took him to be. Darcy, as Elizabeth notes, "improves on acquaintance" and improves even more on acquaintance at his house.[11] At Pemberley, he shows himself to be a man of imagination, discernment, and taste, capable of making those far below his social standing feel welcomed and valued in his home. In other words, he begins to appear to Elizabeth as someone she could genuinely love.

Pemberley's hospitable atmosphere is not a happy accident of fortune; it is a reflection of Darcy's good taste, and warm feelings. Before going to Pemberley, Elizabeth based her assessment of Darcy's moral character on his personal manners, which are certainly flawed. But Pemberley provides her with evidence that his moral capacities are much greater than his manners would imply. Darcy, unlike Lady Catherine, is attuned to the needs, feelings, and desires of his guests, and Pemberley reflects this. It is the house of a man with a proper sensitivity both to beauty itself and to the way in which it is experienced by other people. (For instance, Darcy redecorates a room with the aim of delighting his sister, and succeeds because he understands what she will find beautiful.) Pemberley is proof both of Darcy's moral imagination and his willingness to employ it so as to please other people.

Austen's novels illustrate the ways in which domestic arrangements influence and are influenced by the moral characters of the people who inhabit them. Indeed, in Austen's world, houses and estates are generally reasonably good reflections on the characters of the people who live there. The immensely wealthy, but stupid and socially inept Mr. Rushworth of *Mansfield Park* has a poorly situated and hopelessly old-fashioned estate, with inconveniences around every corner. He can see that Sotherton needs improvements, but he is completely incapable of undertaking them. The day the characters spend at Sotherton is a day during which almost no one is comfortable or at home. It is not all poor Rushworth's fault, but it's also clear that he lacks the moral imagination necessary to be a good host or, for that matter, a good husband. There is nothing especially wrong with his moral principles, but it's clear that Austen intends us to find his character inadequate in important respects. His house reflects his personal deficiencies; he means well, but has no idea what it is that his visitors really want or need.

Austen's novels also have characters, such as Caroline Bingley and Elizabeth Elliot, who have dubious moral characters, but excellent taste. Some of these characters turn out to be villains. But even then, they tend to be villains with moral possibilities. *Mansfield Park*'s Henry Crawford has substantial imaginative capacities; unlike Rushworth, he has the skill necessary to improve an estate and make it truly beautiful. He also has enough moral taste to see the merits of Fanny Price and fall in love with her. Had his moral principles been better, he might have been worthy of her. Alas, his narcissistic, self-indulgent streak eventually does him in, and his considerable talents are wasted.

Elizabeth did doubt Darcy's moral principles, but even once his good character was restored in her eyes, he was not completely redeemed until she visited Pemberley. There she realized that Darcy was not simply a better trained version of Rushworth. Unlike Rushworth, Darcy has good moral taste, something that every single Austen hero has. It is not always recognized as good taste, particularly by those who lack taste themselves. Nowhere is this more apparent than in *Emma*, where the perfect taste of Mr. Knightley's behavior at home and in company is completely lost on the vulgar Mrs. Elton. (Occasionally, it is even lost on Emma, who incorrectly sees as undignified Mr. Knightley's preference for walking to social engagements rather than taking out his carriage.)

In Austen's view, a person's house is an expression both of her moral virtues and also of her moral failings. Some people offer hospitality badly, some offer it well. Some offer the trappings of it well, but lack the warmth to make it genuine. Virtuous hospitality requires both the will to please one's guests and the ability to see and bring about what they will find pleasing. It is the latter ability that I have been describing as good moral taste. A truly virtuous Austenian host must be deeply concerned with his or her guest's welfare and also capable of creating an environment and experience that will foster that welfare. Mr. Woodhouse, Emma's father, is a kind man who cares greatly about his guests and their health. But he lacks the ability (or perhaps the will) to do what they will find pleasing. Believing himself to be acting in their best interests, he offers them gruel when they would rather have cake. Emma, with her greater moral imagination and sensitivity to the needs and desires of her guests, has a much superior capacity for hospitality.

Few of us have the means to display our good taste in the manner of Emma Woodhouse or Darcy or Emily Post's characters, the Oldnames, whose relatively modest house is exquisitely furnished. Luckily, neither Austen nor Post thinks that tasteful hospitality is the sole province of the wealthy, and certainly wealth does not guarantee it. Austen's novels are filled with characters who have limited means but who nevertheless host people graciously. (The Harvilles in *Persuasion* are probably the best example.) And Post's Mrs. Three-in-One is just as capable of offering virtuous hospitality as the Oldnames, even though she does it on a smaller, much less expensive scale.

Virtuous hospitality, then, is fundamentally about the imaginative use of one's resources on behalf of one's guests. If the aim is to please them, a host must be attentive to what his or her guests will find comfortable, pleasant, and beautiful. Creating beauty is, of course, what Martha Stewart does best. And although she is often criticized as upholding a standard of entertaining accessible only to those with wealth and leisure, I think we have good reason to think of her as working in the tradition of Austen and Post, albeit with a twist that will take us back to Aristotle.

Stewart's rise to fame is a fascinating story. The daughter of middle-class Polish-American parents, she grew up learning a wide variety of practical household skills. She graduated from Barnard College with a degree in architectural history, eventually becoming a stockbroker and launching one of the most successful companies in American history. Certainly, Stewart has her critics and her conviction on charges of obstruction of justice obviously casts her moral integrity into doubt. It may be that like Henry Crawford, she has good taste without a good character. But she certainly does have good taste; indeed, it's plausible to think of her as the contemporary embodiment of tasteful hospitality in American culture.

In Chapter 3, I discussed the issue of what makes people like Emily Post and Judith Martin experts in American etiquette. We can ask a similar question about Martha Stewart. Just what is it about Stewart that has made her the standard-bearer for good taste? Why is it that millions of people want to do whatever it is that Martha does? It's true that Stewart has either training or work experience in many of the areas in which she is recognized as an expert. But it is not just her educational background that grounds her authority; plenty of people have that. Rather, as we will see, what Stewart exhibits is a combination of aesthetic insight and practical skill, something that is important to the good taste necessary for virtuous hospitality.

In one of his dialogues, Plato raised the question of whether the gods love what is pious because it is pious, or whether it is pious because the gods love it. This has become known as the Euthyphro problem, after the dialogue in which it appears. A slightly later version asks whether God commands actions because they are good, or whether actions are good because God commands them. The philosophical problem is about the location of the standard of goodness. If whatever God commands is good, then if God commands murder, it would be good. But if God commands what is already good, then there is a standard for goodness outside of God. Either answer leads to problems about the nature of God (the first about God's goodness and the second about God's power). The Martha Stewart phenomenon raises a similar problem about taste. Are things tasteful because Martha says that they are, or does she label them as tasteful because she recognizes them as adhering to some pre-existing standard of beauty or style?

This question about the source of Stewart's authority over good taste is reflected in her trademark concept of a Good Thing.[12] In her magazines, television shows, website and books, Stewart identifies a particular object, activity, or practice and labels it a Good Thing. The actual range of Good Things is considerable, covering everything from plastic bag organizers made from dishtowels to small tables and chairs made from snow. The practice of *mis en place* in cooking (chopping, measuring, and setting aside ingredients in advance of preparing the dish) is a Good

Thing, as is constructing artificial cherry branches out of sticks and vellum paper.

What makes these Good Things good? Is it just because Martha says that they are good, or is there something about the object or practice that makes it good, something that Martha recognizes? If it's the former, then the goodness of the thing depends entirely on Stewart's declaring it to be good. There is some reason to think that this is how her Good Things work. Stewart, like Oprah Winfrey, has a remarkable power to start trends. If she declares Depression-era milk glass vases to be a Good Thing, we can count on the price of milk glass items skyrocketing on eBay. Generally speaking, the mere fact that Martha likes something or does something is sufficient to justify anyone else's having it or doing it. To put it differently, millions of people seem to think that if it's good enough for Martha, it's good enough for the rest of us.

Unsurprisingly, Stewart does not present herself as simply anointing certain objects as good or tasteful. Rather, she suggests that what she is doing is identifying objects or projects that are good according to some standard external to her own judgment. We see this reflected in this explanation of a Good Thing from the introduction to her 1997 book:

> When I started taping our television show almost five years ago, I thought it was very evocative to make the statement "It's a good thing" every time I did something neat, quick, particularly simple, or sensible . . . Now everyone at *Martha Stewart Living* thinks the way I do when attempting to decide what is a "good thing" and what is not. The criteria for a "good thing" are complex, but straightforward. Is the project uncomplicated? Is it useful? Is it aesthetically pleasing? Is it something that many people will find interesting or pertinent to their lifestyle? Is it seasonal in nature? Are the materials used to complete the project easy to find? Is the result unusual?[13]

To some extent, these criteria reflect Hume's (and Post's) emphasis on utility and agreeableness. And some of Stewart's Good Things are clearly useful in some way. Certainly, preparing ingredients in advance is a practical way to cook a complicated meal, particularly when one is likely to be entertaining dinner guests in the kitchen while cooking. It is useful because it enables a host to give more of his attention to his guests while still preparing the meal. Insofar as this is the case, it is something that any good host has reason to do. Stewart was not the first person to think of it, nor does her sanctioning it as a Good Thing imply that it is good only because she says so. For this particular Good Thing, Martha's contribution is mostly to remind us about its utility.

When it comes to other Good Things, however, the value of doing or replicating the Good Thing is more complicated. What makes cherry branches with vellum blossoms—not obviously useful—a good thing for any of us? Here the appeal must be to one of the other criteria, such as aesthetic merit. It is good because it is lovely, but probably only if it really turns out to be lovely. As any reader of Martha Stewart Living knows, the crafts pictured in the magazine have always been completed by someone with a considerable degree of practical skill. Whether my own result will be lovely will depend on the extent to which I have that skill. If I am hopeless with vellum and a glue gun, then my cherry branches will lack the aesthetic appeal that makes them a Good Thing in Stewart's mind.

Stewart's portrayal of Good Things certainly suggests that they are good not just for her, but for all of us. But if I can't make my paper cherry blossoms look like Martha's, as I almost certainly cannot, does that mean that they are not a Good Thing for me? Although she doesn't acknowledge it directly, Stewart's use of Good Thing seems to encompass not just beauty and utility, but also the value of an object as something created by a particular person. The goal is not simply to have something lovely in my house; rather, the goal is to have something lovely that I had a hand in constructing. In this sense, Stewart's craft projects are an expression of a practical skill directly tied to the traditional aims of domesticity.

The ancient Greeks spent a great deal of time talking about *techne*, or craft knowledge. Indeed, Aristotle considered it to be one of the intellectual virtues. *Techne*, like practical wisdom, is oriented toward action. But unlike practical wisdom, the skill of *techne* is derived from features of the object being made. The carpenter displays *techne* when he makes a fine chair. Whether it is a fine chair or not depends on the purpose of a chair and how well it fulfills that purpose.

Stewart herself has an extraordinary range of technical skills and enthusiastically employs them across a wide range of domestic problems. (Because of this, she is an easy subject of parody. Among the most famous is a magazine called *Is Martha Stewart Living?* in which Martha provides instructions for making homemade water and 90-grain bread for guests.) The exercise of *techne* is part of what makes an item like handmade paper cherry branches a Good Thing.

It's true that if I lack Stewart's *techne*, my cherry branches will not look like hers, but what this means in Martha's world is not that I shouldn't undertake the craft project, but that I should acquire the skills needed to make them. This assumption is in the background of Stewart's entire enterprise. For instance, quite a few of Stewart's Good Things require that the creator know how to sew. To that end, the *Good Things* book contains a section on the basics of sewing with a machine. The suggestion is not that non-sewers should just skip those projects; rather, it is that non-sewers should learn how to sew. What it is for something to be a Good Thing in Stewart's sense, then, is to be the exemplification of a kind of practical domestic skill akin to a kind of craft knowledge. The development and exercise of *techne* is fundamental to Martha's conception of virtue in the domestic sphere.

Although her market is clearly middle- and upper-middle-class women with quite a bit of leisure time, there is something downright populist about Martha's vision of domesticity. Stewart's mantra is that anyone is capable of creating beautiful objects, meals, and events, with a little (or a lot of!) skill and guidance. It is the exercise of skill by the creator that gives at least some Good Things their beauty, not money. The source of Martha's authority over taste is not simply that she knows what object belongs in a space or what dish belongs on a table; she also knows how to create the object or dish that belongs there. Moreover, she is willing to show the rest of us how to create it too.

Stewart has been criticized on feminist grounds, on the grounds that the ideal of domesticity she encourages is an ideal that women have been working hard to leave behind. And indeed, Stewart works in what is a very long line of domestic advice-givers in American history.[14] Early authors of domestic advice books were concerned with the physical safety of women and their families, and heavy workloads caused by inefficient systems. Nineteenth-century domestic advisors like Catharine Beecher and her sister, Harriet Beecher Stowe, employed the tools of science in the service of trying to make American homes cleaner and safer. The assumption was that if women were going to be in charge of their homes, they might as well have the tools to do it well.

But in between explanations of food safety and plumbing intricacies, most domestic advice manuals of the past simply took for granted that women's work should be centered around the home. Sometimes this was reinforced by religious or biological arguments about the natural duties and tendencies of women. Modern domestic advice givers like Martha Stewart or Cheryl Mendelson of course do not make such claims.[15] They point out that the domestic skills they explain and advocate are needed by both men and women, that there is nothing essentially feminine about knowing how to make a bed properly or clean a soapstone countertop. Still, it is hard not to think that Stewart, though an extraordinarily successful businesswoman herself, has only made women's lives more difficult by ratcheting up the standards by which women are still usually evaluated.

It is not easy to meet Stewart's or Post's standards for tasteful entertaining and home decorating. Darcy, after all, had not just money, but a great deal of spare time to devote to enhancing the loveliness of Pemberley and perfecting his skills at hosting visitors. Modern men and women do not live that way. Stewart and Mendelson argue that this is unfortunate, that life is simply more pleasant and more beautiful when attention is paid to domestic order and harmony. The stunning success of Stewart's enterprise suggests that many people find that argument convincing.

Stewart claims to be in the business of entertaining, not hospitality, but her claims about what it is that makes something good or tasteful are closely linked to her conception of what is beautiful and useful in a home. On her view, aesthetic appeal is increased by practical skill, perhaps in part because it infuses the object with the personality of the creator. Of course, if I am following Martha's step-by-step instructions, my creation may be as infused with Martha's personality as my own. But this is not something that Martha herself appears to be endorsing. Indeed, I think it makes more sense to see her as following in Post's footsteps in declaring the object or the table setting to be tasteful insofar as it expresses something about the host herself or himself.

Hospitality as a virtue seems to be closely linked with self-sacrifice. Sometimes the sacrifice is considerable, such as when people take in friends or relatives for long periods of time. But if Post and Stewart are right, the appeal of a room decorated by its owner rather than a professional, or a meal cooked by the person who is serving it, is in part based on the sacrifice it represents, the willingness to put oneself out for the sake of one's guests and create what they will find beautiful or pleasing. The placement of a wine glass is not important in itself; what is important is its role in producing an overall effect. Insofar as proper table settings are aesthetically pleasing (or useful because we can always find what we need), they are part of offering hospitality.

It is, of course, possible to take this too far. If I set a beautiful table that intimidates my guests to the point that they cannot enjoy their meal, I am failing to be hospitable. If I am so exhausted from creating cherry blossoms out of vellum that I can't strike up an interesting conversation with my guests, then I've made a major mistake about the requirements of hospitality. In the *Seinfeld* example with which I began this book, Elaine certainly takes the quest for chocolate babka too far. Her obsession with getting what she thinks is the perfect hostess gift completely undermines everything that the evening is supposed to be about. Even if she is correct that it would be in poor taste to bring Pepsi and Ring Dings, it is in even poorer taste to show up at a dinner party in a foul mood. Elaine is not virtuous enough to see this; she is capable of appreciating only the superficialities of good taste. (Elizabeth Bennet would have known better.)

Thus far, I have focused primarily on the practice of offering hospitality. There are, of course, also many etiquette rules about receiving hospitality well. Judith Martin claims, tongue-in-cheek, that it is easy to be the perfect guest: "All you have to do is remember everything you've learned in the last few years about being totally honest, in touch with your feelings, able to communicate your needs and committed to doing what makes you feel comfortable. And then forget it."[16] She exaggerates, but not by much. In Chapter 4, we discussed the importance of tactful guests in maintaining a host's front during a disastrous dinner party. For Martin, receiving hospitality virtuously requires unflagging cheerfulness, consideration, and cooperation, regardless of how difficult that is to manage. Of course, there is a balance to be struck here. A guest who never expresses any preferences about anything can be just as annoying to her host as a guest who makes constant demands. Hosts want their guests to be genuinely comfortable, and part of a guest's responsibility is to help the host make that happen.

In this chapter, I have argued that the virtue of hospitality requires the exercise of moral imagination on behalf of one's guests. Good hosts have the capacity to create an environment and an experience that their guests will find pleasing and that will further the moral aims of friendship and conviviality. Guests, for their part, should accept with good grace the host's efforts to produce that environment and do what is necessary to sustain it.

Of all the twentieth-century etiquette experts, it is probably Lillian Eichler who expressed most clearly what is morally valuable about hospitality:

> For hospitality is that open-hearted, open-handed, generous, lovable, beautiful fellow-feeling for fellow-mortals—the kind of feeling that makes you throw open your home, small apartment or mighty mansion, as the case may be, and bid your friends and acquaintances welcome . . . And so it goes on, a constant giving and returning of hospitality, so beautiful and so inspiring that it is worthy of the stress given to it in the social world.[17]

One can certainly offer the kind of hospitality that Eichler describes without putting together a five-course meal or spending every weekend at flea markets to find just the right vintage tablecloth. But one cannot offer it without a kind of imaginative attentiveness to one's guests and what will please them, or what I have described as a kind of good moral taste. My claim has been that this capacity is essential to offering truly virtuous hospitality. Giving and receiving hospitality of this sort is undoubtedly a Good Thing.

Conclusion

> Trifles are unimportant, it is true, but then life is made up of trifles.[1]
>
> Richard Duffy

The purpose of this book has been to establish and explain the moral value of the trifles that make up our contemporary lives. Of course, if our social customs and conventions have the moral value I have ascribed to them, they are hardly trifles. I hope to have established that the rules of polite behavior play a far more important role in helping us live out our moral commitments than most people realize. They enable us to express and act upon moral ideals like respect, self-respect, and consideration for others. Because of this, they are not simply optional extras. They are part of the practice of morality itself.

In his history of American manners, Arthur Schlesinger describes a shift in our thinking about the relationship between morality and manners:

> At first, politeness was so closely identified with morality as to be scarcely distinguishable. It was then usual to define manners as "minor morals." Lord Chesterfield's writings, however, helped to drive a wedge between the two, a process which reached completion when the middle classes came to the top, intent on aping the ways of those whom they had formerly deemed to be of finer clay. Etiquette now

managed to disentangle itself from ethics, taking on its modern meaning of a generalized pattern of behavior designed to lubricate social intercourse.[2]

In this book, I have argued that etiquette has not in fact disentangled itself from ethics and moreover, that it could not without losing most of its force. Etiquette books that do not take ethical considerations seriously are neither very interesting nor very useful, since it is impossible for their authors to provide the necessary grounding or authority for their claims about what we should do. The question of the point of etiquette can only be answered by turning to the study of morality itself. And likewise, the study of morality is incomplete unless we attend to its manifestation in ordinary human interactions.

The rules of etiquette represent morality in practice. True, they change over time, and they vary from culture to culture. And in our increasingly diverse and technologically sophisticated world, social conventions have perhaps never been more in flux, which is why we need skilled etiquette writers as much as ever. Our manners serve as the language through which we express some of our deepest moral commitments. Learning that language is essential to living a fully human, fully moral life. In the words of Emily Post, "Etiquette is the science of living. It embraces everything."[3]

Notes

ONE INTRODUCTION

1 "The Dinner Party," *Seinfeld*, NBC, originally aired on February 3, 1994.

2 "The Dinner Party."

3 In this book, I will use the terms "morality" and "ethics" interchangeably, as is customary in moral philosophy.

4 Judith Martin, *Miss Manners Rescues Civilization from Sexual Harassment, Frivolous Lawsuits, Dissing, and Other Lapses in Civility* (New York: Crown Publishers, 1996), 11.

5 For an extensive discussion of the role of manners in political contexts, see Peter Johnson, *The Philosophy of Manners* (Bristol: Thoemmes Press, 1999).

6 Thomas Hobbes, *Leviathan*, ed. Michael Oakeshott (New York: Collier, 1962), 100.

7 Although Hobbes does attend to considerations of manners, his "civil society" wouldn't necessarily have been civil in the sense that we use that word. For more about Hobbes on manners, see Peter Johnson, "Hobbes on Human Nature and the Necessity of Manners," *Angelaki*, 3 (1) (1998): 67–76.

8 James Boswell, *The Life of Samuel Johnson*, ed. Charles G. Osgood (Project Gutenberg, 2006), www.gutenberg.org/files/1564/1564-h/1564-h.htm (accessed January 7, 2011).

9 Plato, *The Republic*, trans. G. M. A. Grube, rev. C. D. C. Reeve (Indianapolis: Hackett, 1992). In the dialogue, Glaucon is playing devil's advocate. He himself hopes that the claim is not true, so he asks the character of Socrates to come up with an argument against it.

10 Notoriously, Kant believed that animals count as objects, which is not the way that we usually think of at least some animals. This is not because Kant hated animals; rather, it's because his theory leaves space for only two categories—ends in themselves and objects. Insofar as animals aren't rational, they can't be ends. Kant's ethics is often criticized on these grounds.

11 Not everybody thinks this, of course. Contemporary defenses of civility and manners have been offered by Stephen Carter, Civility (New York: HarperCollins, 1998); Gertrude Himmelfarb, The De-Moralization of Society (New York: Vintage Books, 1994); P. M. Forni, Choosing Civility (New York: St. Martin's Griffin, 2002); and Leroy Rouner, ed., Civility (Notre Dame, IN: Notre Dame Press, 2000).

12 Notable exceptions within philosophy include the following: Sarah Buss, "Appearing Respectful: The Moral Significance of Manners," Ethics, 109 (1999): 795–826; Cheshire Calhoun, "The Virtue of Civility," Philosophy and Public Affairs, 29 (2000): 251–275; Nancy Sherman, "Manners and Morals," in Stoic Warriors (Oxford: Oxford University Press, 2005); Peter Johnson, The Philosophy of Manners (Bristol: Thoemmes Press, 1999). Mark Caldwell approaches the subject of manners from the standpoint of cultural studies in A Short History of Rudeness (New York: Picador, 1999).

13 Lord Chesterfield, Letters, ed. David Roberts (Oxford: Oxford University Press, 1992), 137.

14 The version in use is from the Oxford Illustrated Jane Austen series, ed. R. W. Chapman, 3rd ed. (Oxford: Oxford University Press). All references to Austen's novels in this book are from this series. This scene from Pride and Prejudice takes place on pages 174–176.

15 Austen, Pride and Prejudice, 225.

TWO THE LINK BETWEEN MORALITY AND MANNERS

1 Mark Twain's Helpful Hints for Good Living: A Handbook for the Damned Human Race, ed. Lin Salamo, Victor Fischer, and Michael B. Frank (Berkeley: University of California Press, 2004), 30.

2 For a discussion of etiquette and morality in terms of hypothetical and categorical imperatives, see Philippa Foot, "Morality as a System of Hypothetical Imperatives," Philosophical Review, 81 (3) (1972): 305–316.

3 Judith Martin, Miss Manners: A Citizen's Guide to Civility (New York: Three Rivers Press, 1999), 24–25.

4 This is not to say that it is absolutely binding. There can be good reasons for violating etiquette rules.

5 Ibid., 25.

6 David Hume, Enquiry Concerning the Principles of Morals, ed. Tom Beauchamp (Oxford: Clarendon Press, 1998), 67. For a specific discussion of Hume on manners, see Peter Johnson, "Hume on Manners and the Civil Condition," British Journal of the History of Philosophy, 6 (2) (1998): 209–222.

7 There are actually many different versions of utilitarianism. The version I'm describing is often known as classical act-utilitarianism. It was made

famous by Jeremy Bentham in the late eighteenth century, and has been influential within economics and public policy.

8 Buss, "Appearing Respectful," 802.

9 There are, of course, other ways of conveying respect when making a request, such as using a certain tone of voice. I am grateful to an anonymous reviewer for reminding me of this point.

10 Martin Luther King, Jr., "Letter from a Birmingham Jail," The Martin Luther King Jr. Research and Education Institute, Stanford University, www.stanford.edu/group/King/frequentdocs/birmingham.pdf (accessed January 7, 2011).

11 Martin, Miss Manners Rescues Civilization, 19.

12 Martin, Citizen's Guide to Civility, 4.

13 This is a widespread story about Queen Victoria, but I have encountered versions of it with other famous figures in the lead role.

14 This is the strategy recommended by Peggy Post in Emily Post's Etiquette, 16th ed. (New York: HarperCollins, 1997), 153.

15 One of the better known books on intercultural etiquette is Norine Dresser's Multicultural Manners, 2nd ed. (New Jersey: John Wiley & Sons, 2005). For a brief, but interesting comparison of customs in different countries, see Michael Powell, Behave Yourself! The Essential Guide to International Etiquette (Connecticut: Globe Pequot Press, 2005).

16 For a fascinating look at how the norms of different American subcultures affect the way in which people engage in conversation, see Deborah Tannen, Conversational Style, 2nd ed. (Oxford: Oxford University Press, 2005).

THREE   ETIQUETTE EXPERTISE

1 Dorothy Parker, "Mrs. Post Enlarges on Etiquette," review of Etiquette, by Emily Post, New Yorker, December 31, 1927.

2 "The Wire," Curb Your Enthusiasm, HBO, originally aired on November 19, 2000.

3 Laura Claridge, Emily Post (New York: Random House, 2009), 430.

4 Emily Post, Etiquette, 7th ed. (New York: Funk and Wagnalls, 1942), ix.

5 Ibid., x.

6 Unfortunately for Post, her husband did not abide by this rule. His many affairs and the blackmail that ensued made Post and her marriage tabloid fodder in 1905. Post appears never to have forgiven him for exposing her to that kind of public humiliation.

7 Emily Post, Etiquette, 7th ed., x–xi.

8 Claridge, Emily Post, 262–265.

9 Emily Post, *Etiquette*, 2.

10 Hume, *Enquiry*, 67.

11 What counts as an invitation is itself a tricky topic, and one that occupies quite a few column inches in the world of etiquette advice. In particular, people disagree over whether invitations issued via Facebook or invitations to parties that are actually fundraisers or sales events fall under this rule.

12 Emily Post, *Etiquette*, 7th ed., 353–354.

13 Immanuel Kant, *The Metaphysics of Morals*, trans. Mary Gregor (Cambridge: Cambridge University Press, 1991), 209. I am grateful to an anonymous reviewer for reminding me of this passage.

14 Aristotle, *Nicomachean Ethics*, trans. Terence Irwin, 2nd ed. (Indianapolis: Hackett, 1999).

15 Aristotle's ideas about developmental moral psychology are now quite outdated, but we'll ignore that for the moment.

16 Aristotle, *Nicomachean Ethics*, 97.

17 Martin, for all her many virtues, does not, I think, fully appreciate the conceptual complexities of text message conversations. I say more about this in the next chapter.

18 Judith Martin, *Miss Manners' Guide to Excruciatingly Correct Behavior*, 2nd ed. (New York: W. W. Norton and Company, 2005), 556–557.

19 Ibid., 557.

20 Ibid., 557.

21 Ibid., 557.

22 Judith Martin, *Guide for the Turn of the Millennium* (New York: Simon & Schuster, 1990), 176–177.

23 Lord Chesterfield, *Letters*, 20–21.

24 Ibid., 43.

25 Observing too much, of course, can devolve into nosiness. I am grateful to Elijah Milgram for pushing me on this point.

26 Thus, if I know you never go to bed before midnight and don't mind getting late night phone calls, it's not rude to call you at 11:30.

27 Judith Martin, *Guide to Domestic Tranquility* (New York: Crown Publishers, 1999), 129.

28 Dorothy Parker, "Mrs. Post Enlarges on Etiquette."

FOUR SELF-PRESENTATION

1 Jane Austen, *Emma*, 119.

2 For an excellent discussion of the point of secrecy in general, see Sissela Bok, *Secrets* (New York: Vintage Books, 1989).

3 Emily Post, *Etiquette*, 7th ed., 623.

4 For an interpretation that sees Wharton as endorsing (at least in part) the norms of propriety represented by May, see D. Z. Phillips, *Through a Darkening Glass* (South Bend, IN: University of Notre Dame, 1982), 20–21. I am grateful to Peter Johnson for pointing me to this.

5 Immanuel Kant, *Lectures on Ethics*, trans. Louis Infield (Indianapolis: Hackett, 1963), 224–225.

6 Judith Martin, *Citizen's Guide to Civility*, 13.

7 Immanuel Kant, *Lectures on Ethics*, 225.

8 Ibid., 206.

9 Ibid., 224.

10 Erving Goffman, *The Presentation of the Self in Everyday Life* (New York: Anchor Books, 1959), 22.

11 Sam Gosling, *Snoop: What Your Stuff Says About You* (Philadelphia, PA: Basic Books, 2008).

12 Goffman, *Presentation of the Self*, 231–232.

13 Ibid., 170.

14 Ibid., 128.

15 Gosling, *Snoop*, 132.

16 Kant, *The Metaphysics of Morals*, 222–223.

17 Kant, *Lectures on Ethics*, 118.

18 Kant, *Metaphysics of Morals*, 258.

19 Ibid., 262.

20 Erving Goffman, "Embarrassment and Social Organization," in *Interaction Ritual* (New York: Pantheon Books, 1967), 102–103.

21 J. Suler, "The Online Disinhibition Effect," *CyberPsychology and Behavior*, 7 (2004): 321–326.

FIVE   POLITE LIES

1 Ludwig Wittgenstein, *Culture and Value*, trans. Peter Winch (Chicago: University of Chicago Press), 64e.

2 Sissela Bok suggests that it makes an enormous difference to these totals whether we count non-statements as lies. See her book, *Lying*, 2nd ed. (New York: Vintage Books, 1999), xxiii.

3 Some of them, most notably Socrates, denied that there is such a thing as weakness of will. Socrates held that all wrongdoing is a form of ignorance. To know the good is to do it; hence, anyone who doesn't do what is good must be lacking in some kind of knowledge.

4 *The Encyclopedia of Etiquette: A Guide to Good Manners in Today's World* (New York: Crown Publishers, 1967), 367.

5 *Vogue's Book of Etiquette* (New York: Simon and Schuster, 1948), 44.

6 Emily Post, *Etiquette*, 7th ed., 624.

7 Ibid., 624.

8 She does note that "when the motive is self-advantage, then tact and truth are apt to part company" (ibid., 623). This, of course, was the worry expressed about Lord Chesterfield's advice, that he was recommending tact for self-interested reasons alone.

9 Hugo Grotius, *On the Law of War and Peace*, trans. Francis W. Kelsey (New York: Bobbs-Merrill Co., 1925), bk. 3, ch. 1, sect. XI.

10 It is actually quite difficult to pin down Kant's views about lying. He is more lenient about lying in the *Lectures on Ethics* than in his more famous (and later) essay, "On a Supposed Right to Lie from Philanthropic Concerns" (Indianapolis: Hackett, 1993). In the *Metaphysics of Morals*, he takes a fairly strong stand against lying. But he also poses a "casuistical" question about whether polite lies can be justified, suggesting that he does not see the topic as fully decided. Moreover, it's hard to know exactly what Kant considered to be a lie in the first place. For more on this topic, see Allen Wood, "Lies," in *Kantian Ethics* (Cambridge: Cambridge University Press, 2008); Christine Korsgaard, "The Right to Lie: Kant on Dealing with Evil" and "Two Arguments Against Lying," in *Creating the Kingdom of Ends* (Cambridge: Cambridge University Press, 1996); James Mahon, "Kant and the Perfect Duty to Others Not to Lie," *British Journal for the History of Philosophy*, 14 (2006): 653–685.

11 Kant, "On a Supposed Right to Lie." Wood ("Lies") suggests that the case under discussion is a highly unusual situation, one in which the would-be murderer actually has some authority to extract a truthful declaration from the unfortunate person who answers the door. If he is right, then Kant's claim here is much less contentious than it has generally been taken to be.

12 Kant says this quite explicitly in the *Lectures on Ethics* (227) and suggests it in "On a Supposed Right to Lie" (64).

13 On the Augustinian view of lying, see Paul Griffiths, *Lying: An Augustinian Theology of Duplicity* (Michigan: Brazos Press, 2004).

14 See Wood, "Lies," *Kantian Ethics*; James Mahon, "Kant on Lies, Candour, and Reticence," *Kantian Review*, 7 (2003): 102–133.

15 *Summa Theologiae*, II–II, q. 110, a 2. Thomas Aquinas is one of history's earliest and primary proponents of what is known as natural law theory in ethics. For a contemporary version of natural law ethics, see Mark Murphy, *Natural Law and Practical Rationality* (Cambridge: Cambridge University Press, 2001).

16 Officious and jocose lies are generally venial sins at most, whereas mischievous lies are mortal sins.

17 For a different view, see Thomas L. Carson, *Lying and Deception: Theory and Practice* (Oxford: Oxford University Press, 2010).

18 Broadening it is more controversial than restricting it.

19 Judith Martin, *Miss Manners' Basic Training: The Right Thing to Say* (New York: Crown Publishers, 1998), 48–49.

20 Ibid., 49.

21 At least he does in his later work. In his earlier work, he seems slightly more charitably disposed toward the practice of mental reservation.

22 Emily Post, *Etiquette*, 7th ed., 623.

23 Ibid., 624.

24 Kant, *Metaphysics of Morals*, 225.

25 "Dear Prudence: Lap Dance Led to Engagement," *Slate*, V, www.slatev. com/video/dear-prudence-lap-dance-led-engagement, originally aired on December 9, 2010.

SIX GIVING AND RECEIVING

1 "Gifts," in *The Essential Writings of Ralph Waldo Emerson*, ed. Brooks Atkinson (New York: Modern Library, 2000), 361.

2 Michael Rosenwald, "Amazon Patents Procedure to Let Recipients Avoid Undesirable Gifts," *Washington Post*, December 27, 2010, A1.

3 See Marcel Mauss, *The Gift*, trans. W. D. Halls (New York: W. W. Norton, 1990).

4 There can, of course, be professional contexts in which someone may have a right to my advice, perhaps because she has paid me a retainer.

5 Martin, *Guide to Domestic Tranquility*, 285.

6 There are often different conventions for attendants.

7 I have benefited from discussions with Tony Manela about the moral status of favors.

8 One of the many confusing things about Kant's ethical theory is that it employs the concept of an end in two very different ways. Rational beings are ends in themselves, but rational beings also set ends for themselves. Ends in the latter sense are more like commitments, projects, or goals.

9 Kant, *Metaphysics of Morals*, 244.

10 Peter Singer, "Famine Affluence, and Morality," *Philosophy and Public Affairs*, 1 (1) (1972): 229–243.

11 An anonymous reviewer has raised the concern that etiquette rules can hold back necessary social changes. People may be motivated to change their gift-giving practices, but feel bound by the rules of etiquette to give traditional gifts anyway. Of course, it can go the other direction as well, as the example of Emily Post declaring chaperones unnecessary shows. (See Chapter 3.)

12 Martin, *Guide for the Turn of the Millennium*, 515.

13 "The Labelmaker," *Seinfeld*, NBC, originally aired January 19, 1995. In Tim Whatley's defense, the label maker was defective, although that means his gift to Jerry was pretty shoddy.

14 There can be exceptions. Martin notes that one must refuse a diamond bracelet from a gentleman one barely knows, but this needn't mean that one isn't grateful.

15 See Mauss, *The Gift*.

16 Kant, *Metaphysics of Morals*, 247.

17 Martin, *Guide to Excruciatingly Correct Behavior*, 616. Presumably she is being sarcastic about the diamonds.

SEVEN NEIGHBORS

1 "Funkhouser's Crazy Sister," *Curb Your Enthusiasm*, HBO, originally aired on September 20, 2009.

2 Austen, *Pride and Prejudice*, 364.

3 *Parerga and Paralipomena*, trans. E. F. M. Payne (Oxford: Oxford University Press, 2001).

4 Erving Goffman, *Behavior in Public Places* (New York: The Free Press, 1963), 84.

5 At least one study has cast doubt on whether this actually happens in practice. See Mark Cary, "Does Civil Inattention Occur in Pedestrian Passing?" *Journal of Personality and Social Psychology*, 36 (11) (1978): 1185–1193.

6 Goffman, *Behavior in Public Places*, 85.

7 Ibid., 95.

8 M. Zuckerman, M. Miserandino, and F. Bernieri, "Civil Inattention Exists—In Elevators," *Personality and Social Psychology Bulletin*, 9 (4) (December 1983): 578–586.

9 Martin, *Guide to Excruciatingly Correct Behavior*, 137.

10 Goffman, *Behavior in Public Places*, 132–133.

11 Martin, *Guide to Domestic Tranquility*, 320.

12 Post, *Etiquette*, 7th ed., 621.

13 Of course not everyone cares about presenting this particular front. The extent to which we should pretend not to see our neighbors in pajamas depends on the extent to which this front matters to them.

EIGHT HOSPITALITY AND TASTE

1 Martin, *Guide to Domestic Tranquility*, 259.

2 The word itself has been in use for quite some time, at least since the early nineteenth century.

3 Hume, *Enquiry*, 33.

4 Emily Post, *The Personality of a House* (New York: Funk & Wagnalls, 1948), 50.

5 Ibid., 49.

6 Ibid., 6.

7 Austen, *Pride and Prejudice*, 245.

8 Ibid., 373.

9 Ibid., 246.

10 Ibid., 246.

11 Ibid., 234.

12 I am grateful to Gaby Sakamoto for first pointing out to me the philosophical dimensions of this phrase.

13 Martha Stewart, *Good Things* (New York: Clarkson Potter Publishers, 1997), 9.

14 On the history of domestic advice, see Susan Strasser, *Never Done* (New York: Pantheon Books, 1982); Sarah A. Leavitt, *From Catharine Beecher to Martha Stewart* (Chapel Hill: University of North Carolina Press, 2002); Barbara Ehrenreich and Deirdre English, *For Her Own Good*, 2nd ed. (New York: Anchor Books, 2005).

15 Martha Stewart, *Martha Stewart's Homekeeping Handbook* (New York: Clarkson Potter, 2006); Cheryl Mendelson, *Home Comforts* (New York: Scribner, 1999).

16 Martin, *Guide to Excruciatingly Correct Behavior*, 274.

17 Lillian Eichler, *Book of Etiquette*, vol. 1 (New York: Doubleday, 1921), 285.

CONCLUSION

1 Richard Duffy, introduction to *Etiquette*, by Emily Post (New York: Funk & Wagnalls, 1922), xxvi.

2 Arthur M. Schlesinger, *Learning How to Behave* (New York: Coopers Square Publishers, 1968), 64–65.

3 As quoted on The Emily Post Institute's website, www.emilypost.com/guidelines-for-living/454-emily-post-quotations, accessed on January 10, 2011.

Credits

I am grateful to the Emily Post Institute for granting me permission to reprint parts of the 7th edition of Emily Post's *Etiquette* (New York: Funk and Wagnalls, 1942) and *The Personality of a House* (New York: Funk & Wagnalls, 1948).